Them

C000184063

Other books by the author
available from Marshall Pickering

ASSEMBLY PRAISE
QUOTATIONS FOR ALL OCCASIONS

Themes for Family Worship

Using the NIV and Junior Praise

TONY CASTLE

Marshall Pickering
An Imprint of HarperCollins*Publishers*

First published in Great Britain in 1992 by Marshall Pickering

Marshall Pickering is an imprint of
HarperCollins*Religious*
Part of HarperCollins*Publishers*
77–85 Fulham Palace Road
Hammersmith, London W6 8JB

Copyright © 1992 Tony Castle

9 8 7 6 5 4 3 2 1

The Author asserts the moral right to
be identified as the author of this work

Printed in Great Britain by HarperCollins Manufacturing, Glasgow

A catalogue record for this book is available from the British Library

ISBN 0 551 02477 1

CONDITIONS OF SALE
This book is sold subject to the condition that it shall not, by way of
trade or otherwise, be lent, re-sold, hired out or otherwise circulated
without the publisher's prior consent in any form of binding or cover other
than that in which it is published and without a similar condition including
this condition being imposed on the subsequent purchaser.

Bible passages are taken from the New International Version of the Bible (NIV)
copyright © 1978 by New York International Bible Society and used by
their permission and that of Hodder & Stoughton, London

Dedicated to
Dilys and Ted

CONTENTS

ACKNOWLEDGEMENTS

The author and publishers would like to thank the following publishers and copyright holders for the use of the material of which they are the copyright holders:

Hodder and Stoughton for the texts from the New International Version of the Bible. Oxford University Press for several short extracts from *Winding Quest, the heart of the Old Testament*, and *New World, the heart of the New Testament*, by Alan Dale. Mowbrays, a Cassell imprint, for the poem by Hsi Sin-Mor, published in 1991.

Every effort has been made to trace the owners of copyright material, where this applies, and it is hoped that no copyright has been infringed. Apology is made if the contrary is shown to be the case and correction will be made by the publishers at the first convenient opportunity.

INTRODUCTION

The Good News is for all but, as every minister knows, proclaiming it to young children, week by week, is a daunting task. Children today live in such a stimulating Technicolor world, where instant interest and pleasure is expected, and where the plain spoken word fails to hold them for long. Hearing alone is soon regarded as 'boring'; from their experiences at school, children expect their other senses to be engaged. They expect to be actively involved in their own learning. Most ministers, who are qualified, biblically and theologically, to preach are not trained to meet the needs of the 4- to 11-year-olds in front of them on a Sunday. Even those who feel comfortable with the challenge are in constant need of fresh material and ideas.

This book is not presented as a handbook answer to one hundred and one weeks of the children's services; it is offered as an aid. Ideally the themes should not be used as prepackaged, ready to serve up to the youngsters; but as skeletal outlines and ideas that can be personalized and developed to suit the occasion, the personality of the preacher and the individual needs of the group to be addressed.

Realistically, the themes will, on occasion, be used with little time for advance preparation; this has been kept in mind in their construction. The suggested materials have been kept simple and easily available, with no or very little time required for preparatory work with the children.

The prayer focus places emphasis upon gratitude to God, which is only then followed by petition. The hymns are all taken from *Junior Praise** and are merely suggested titles that will suit the theme.

A further balance that the compiler has tried to keep in mind is that this book will be used by ministers of differing traditions, who put their emphasis in proclaiming Christ's Good News in slightly different places and ways. As an aid, like a First Aid pack in your home or car, you must, of course, select what is of value and leave aside that which does not meet the need.

It is my hope that much will be of value in meeting one of the most important tasks before ministers today, namely leading children in relevant and stimulating worship.

TONY CASTLE
Harvest 1991

Themes for
Family Worship

THEME: *Accepting Responsibility*

AIM: To help the children begin to understand that they must learn to accept responsibility for what they do wrong, and as a step towards an appreciation of the saving work of the Lord.

AIDS: *Two large cards with the words, "It's not my fault" and "It's not fair" printed on them.*

LEADER: Hands up all those who have ever said these words, (*hold up card and read*): "It's not fair." (*Allow children to give you examples*). Yes, it is something that we hear very often. We feel that it is not fair when we are blamed for something we have not done.

What about these words (*hold up second card*): "It's not my fault" . . . ? Have you ever said them when you shouldn't have done? Now let's be honest and fair, because it is not right to be unfair and we must be honest because God knows the truth. Isn't it true that most of the time you say, "It's not my fault" when you know very well that you did do the wrong thing? . . . it was your fault. You just do not want to take the blame. You blame someone or something else. Is that fair? Is that honest?

One sign of being grown-up, really mature, is to be fair and say, "Yes, I did it, I was wrong and I am sorry." Think about that and stop yourself saying, "It's not my fault" when it really is.

What would you think of a friend who, when you

14

BIBLE TEXT: *Blessed are they whose ways are blameless*
Psalm 119:1

did something wrong, took the blame for you?

For example, you are playing around and something gets broken, your mother (or perhaps a teacher) arrives and sees the broken object at your feet. You say, "It's not my fault, it fell off the shelf." Your friend steps forward and says, "I accept the blame". That is why we love and respect Jesus so much, he did no wrong but took the blame for us. That led to his painful death on the cross.

PRAYER
FOCUS:
Thank you for the love of Jesus who took the blame for all our wrong-doing; help us to have the courage to own up and take the blame when we have done wrong. May we always be fair and not pass the blame on to others.

MUSIC:
Father, lead me day by day   JP43
Just as I am, your child to be   JP146/MP396
May the mind of Christ my Saviour   JP165/MP463

THEME: *Advent*

AIM: To help the children understand the word "Advent" and prepare for the coming birthday of Jesus.

AIDS: *You will need to "borrow" a mother with a new baby, the younger the better. (It is advisable to seek a mother who already has a child or children, because such a mother is usually not so anxious about strangers touching her baby.)*

LEADER: Have any of you got an Advent calendar in your home?

Do you know what the word "Advent" means? Yes, it means, "coming". The birthday of Jesus is coming. But it is much more than that; it reminds us of the long wait the Chosen People had for the appearing of the Messiah or Christ.

(The mother and baby need to be some long distance from the children.)

Over there you can see a mother with her baby and in a moment I am going to ask her to come to you.

Who would like to touch the baby? Yes, don't get excited, you all can in a moment.

Now wait. . . . *(Pause.)*

(Invite the mother to walk very slowly to the children; stop her before she arrives.)

Now you are all anticipating the baby arriving. . . . I can see that some of your can hardly wait.

Now you know the meaning of Advent. . . .

waiting for the coming of the baby Jesus. (*Mother presents the child's head to be touched and stroked; she leaves after a few minutes.*)

PRAYER
FOCUS:
That we may prepare well for the birth of Jesus; and be loving and kind to all babies and young children.

MUSIC:
Hark the glad sound! the Saviour comes   JP68/MP210
O come, O come Emmanuel   JP177/MP493
Come and praise the Lord our King   JP34

And Then

AIM: To help the children look beyond the present moment and consider the possible future effects of their actions.

AIDS: *Two cards, on one the word AND and on the second the word THEN.*

LEADER: Hands up those who can tell me what temptation is. Yes, it is the thought that creeps into our mind that it would be a good thing to do something . . . but deep down we know that the "something", like telling a lie, is wrong. If we do the wrong thing then, of course, we do something which is called a sin.

Here is a little traditional story from Italy.

A bright young man very pleased with his success at college was telling a wise old gentleman about his plans for the future. "I am going to go to university and get a degree in Law." "And then?" asked the old man. "I shall work hard and become a respected and famous lawyer," replied the student. "And then?" the old man enquired. "Well, I suppose I shall marry and have a family and live in a big house." "And then?" asked the old gentleman. "I will become rich, and lots of famous people will want me to be their lawyer." "And then?" the question came again. "Then, well, then I suppose I will get older and eventually retire . . . but of course,

Teach me knowledge and good judgement
                              Psalm 119:66

everyone who is important will know me." "And then?" the old man repeated. The young man was getting irritable. "What do you mean by that?" "I mean," said the elderly gentleman, "what happens next?" "Well, I suppose I will die," came the reply. "And then?" persisted the old man. There was silence; the young man had no answer. "Surely," said the wise old man, "now we come to the important part; how will your story end? In heaven or the other place?"

(*Leader holds up the two cards, one in each hand*). AND, life goes on and on; there is always an AND. THEN, everything we do causes something else to happen. For example, you are asked, "Where have you been?" And you tell a lie. AND THEN (*hold up cards*) you have to tell another one to cover up and so on. Or, someone takes jewellery from a store; AND THEN a store detective stops that person; AND THEN the police arrive; AND THEN the parents are called; AND THEN . . . So before doing anything that you are tempted to do, try the AND THEN test. What will be the results of what you do?

PRAYER
FOCUS:

Gratitude for the love and guidance, as we grow up, of parents, teachers, friends etc; help to consider the AND THEN of all that we do.

MUSIC:

Father, lead me day by day   JP43
Don't build your house   JP39
Father, I place into your hands   JP42/MP133

Anxiety

AIM: To help the children appreciate that all the rush and stress of modern life can be harmful to our Christian life.

AIDS: *An alarm clock, set to go off during the early part of the presentation; cooking utensils, carpet sweeper, etc. A reader.*

LEADER: What have we here? (*Examine the collection of items.*) A clock. Well, grown-ups are always rushing to make up time, to be on time, to save time and so on. The clock seems to control their lives. It doesn't control your lives, does it?

READER: Jesus said, "Unless you become like little children, you shall not enter the Kingdom of Heaven."

LEADER: You see these cooking utensils – saucepans, casserole dish, frying pans and so on. Do your parents spend a lot of time cooking and preparing meals? I expect most of you would prefer something simple, wouldn't you?

READER: Jesus said, "Unless you become like little children, you shall not enter the Kingdom of Heaven."

LEADER: Now here we have a carpet cleaner; how many of you have used one of these? Do you think that there are some grown-ups who use one of these too often? They are always cleaning? Which of you has an untidy bedroom?

BIBLE TEXT:
BIBLE TEXT: *Martha was distracted by all the preparations that had to be made. She came to Jesus and asked, "Lord, don't you care that my sister has left me to do the work . . . ?" "Martha, Martha, you are worried and upset about many things."* Luke 10:40

READER: Jesus said, "Unless you become like little children, you shall not enter the Kingdom of Heaven." (*Etc.*)

LEADER: Jesus told us not to worry and be full of anxiety. If we are simple and trusting, just as little children are, we will not be full of anxiety. Giving time to one another, and listening to one another is acting more like Jesus himself, than tearing around, fretting and anxious about all the things that Martha was worrying about.

PRAYER FOCUS: *Gratitude for our nice homes and the caring people about us; help to be more trusting, leaving things to the loving providence of God.*

MUSIC: Make me a channel of your peace   JP161/MP456
May the mind of Christ my Saviour   JP165/MP463
Turn your eyes upon Jesus   JP260/MP712
(*see also Trust in God*)

Bad Habits

AIM: To help the children understand themselves a little
            more and try to improve their relationship with
            God and one another.

AIDS: *A house brick and a sheet of wood at least five feet in
            length. This should be propped up, like a slide, in view.*

LEADER: What will happen if I place this brick at the top of
            this slide? Yes, it will slide down. (*Match action to
            words.*) Now as it is sliding down, is it easy to stop?
            No, you are quite right it is possible, but not easy.
            (*Match action to words.*)

            The same thing happens if you are on a slide; if
            you are sliding down and then try to grab hold of
            the sides to stop, it is possible, but not very easy.

            Let us read again the opening words from St
            Paul. He is talking about a bad habit: a wrong thing
            that he does which he wants to stop doing, because
            he knows it's wrong; but cannot stop.

            (*Text read.*)
            Have you ever had that experience? You know its
            wrong to cheek your mother or father, you don't
            want to do it, but the words still come out.

            That is something that we must struggle with and
            most of all we must ask God to give us the strength
            to fight such a bad habit. We can change, if we keep
            trying and rely on God for help.

BIBLE TEXT: *I do not understand what I do. For what I want to do I do not do but what I hate, I do.* Romans 7:15

PRAYER
FOCUS: *Thanksgiving for a loving Father who will always help us, if we ask; help to overcome our bad habits and sins.*

MUSIC: Your ways are higher than mine   JP295
When the road is rough and steep   JP279
Father, lead me day by day   JP43
Father, I place into your hands   JP42/MP133

THEME: *Being Whole*

AIM: To help the children appreciate the need to try, all the time, to be better people.

AIDS: *Decorating tools, including sandpaper, filler, etc.*

LEADER: When I decorate a room in my home I first of all use this tool (*show the tool*) to strip off the wallpaper. Then I use this tool and this filler to fill up all the cracks that I can find. When that is finished I sand the paintwork, that is the wood parts that are painted.

All this preparation work is important and has to be done very carefully before I can put up new wallpaper or do the painting.

When all the work is finished the room looks lovely and complete. Every building needs to be repaired or decorated from time to time. The apostle Paul says that we are like a building, a temple; we need to repair the cracks and sand off the lumps and bumps so that we can be lovely and bright, and complete again.

We do that by telling God we are sorry for what we have done wrong, and asking him to fill us with his love and help so that we can be whole and complete persons again.

BIBLE TEXT: *Don't you know that you yourselves are God's temple and that God's Spirit lives in you?* 1 Corinthians 3:16

PRAYER
FOCUS:
Gratitude for God's constant care and willingness to help us make a new start when we are sorry for doing wrong; understanding of our need, every day, to be better people.

MUSIC:
Put you hand in the hand of the man
    who stilled the water   JP206
God forgave my sin in Jesus' name   JP54/MP181
May the mind of Christ my Saviour   JP165/MP463
(*see also Forgiveness*)

The Bible – God's Library

AIM: To develop the children's understanding of the Bible as the word of God.

AIDS: *The following (or similar) jokey "book titles" given to four children prepared to read them out.*

Easy Money by Robin Banks
Hair Care by Dan Druff
Dog's Dinner by Nora Bone
Long Walk by Miss D. Bus

A Bible.

LEADER: Books are important. We learn from them; we enjoy stories from them. We have four amusing titles for you now. (*Titles read out*).

You know what a library is, don't you? Well, here is a puzzle for you. Which book is not a book but a library? (*Accept different suggestions, then, holding up a Bible to view, continue.*)

This looks like a book and we treat it as a book but actually it is a collection of books, it is a type of library. (*Open a few prepared places and read.*)

Listen to this, here is the beginning of the First Book of Kings. At the start of the Bible we have the Book of Genesis, the Book of Proverbs, etc.

Here in the front of the Bible it gives a list of all the books; some are history books, some are poetry, some are hymns and letters.

All of them share something very important; we

*Your word is a lamp to my feet
and a light for my path.*
Psalm 119:101

believe that each one is the word of God. That means we believe that each book of the Bible contains truth from God; God "speaks" to us through the words of these books.

PRAYER
FOCUS:
Thanksgiving for the Bible, God's word to us; help to grow in knowledge and love of God's word.

MUSIC:
The best book to read is the Bible   JP234
Tell me the stories of Jesus   JP228/MP629
Tell me the old, old story   JP227/MP628
(*see also The Bible – God's Word*)

THEME: *The Bible –*
God's Word

AIM: To help the children appreciate that the Bible is much more than a special book with boring readings.

AIDS: *A cardboard cut-out of a crossing sign or perhaps the real thing from a school crossing control person. A Bible.*

LEADER: (*Leader produces the sign, which has been out of sight.*) "STOP. You can cross the road safely here."

Who has to stop when they see this sign? Yes, the cars and all the traffic. Who says they have to stop? The answer is the law of this country, which you can find in a book called *The Highway Code*.

There are other signs that say STOP, but what person makes the traffic stop? Yes, a police officer. Road signs and the police have authority behind them. (*Hold up a large Bible.*) This book has authority behind it too. A much greater authority than the law of our country, it is the authority of God.

In the Old Testament God sent special messengers to his people to say STOP; but they did not always take any notice. The Bible tells about how Jesus came and he did not say STOP, he said, "Love one another."

As we would listen to the word of a policeman, so much more should we listen to the word of God.

BIBLE TEXT: *For the word of God is living and active.*
Sharper than any double-edged sword . . . it
judges the thoughts and attitudes of the heart.

Hebrews 4:12

PRAYER
FOCUS

Thanksgiving for the Bible, God's word to us; help to
listen to and respect God's word.

MUSIC: I am so glad that
our Father in heaven
JP88
Jesus loves me!
this I know
JP140
Make the Book
live to me,
O Lord   JP163
(see also The Bible
– God's Library)

29

Caring

AIM: To help the children associate the word "love" with
         caring and concern for people, as distinct from its
         other meanings.

AIDS: *Six posters prepared, and issued to six of the children.
         On one side carrying one of the captions below and on the
         reverse the letters, C A R I N G*
             "Love is . . . helping at home"
             "Love is . . . sticking up for a friend"
             "Love is . . . keeping a friend's secret"
             "Love is . . . owning up when we are wrong"
             "Love is . . . giving up your last sweet"
             "Love is . . . being patient with a young brother"
         These can, of course, be adapted to local needs.

LEADER: (*Remember who has the letters in order to get them in the
         correct order.*) Let us think about caring and look at
         our first poster. If you care at home by helping you
         show your love . . . (*First poster, with C on the reverse
         side. Child holds the caption to view.*)

         Our friends are important to us (*second poster is
         brought out and stands beside the first one*) so by
         sticking up for a friend we show that we love them.

         If we are to be trusted, and that is part of love,
         (*third poster comes out*) we must be able to keep a
         friend's secret. (*The same process continues until all
         posters are on view.*)

         Love is all about caring for people. Let us see

BIBLE TEXT: *Love is patient, love is kind.*
                              1 Corinthians 13:4

                        what we have on the back of our posters. (*Posters are
                        turned round to spell out CARING*)

PRAYER   *Gratitude for all those who care for us, especially parents*
FOCUS: *and other family members; help to be more caring in our*
                lives at home and at school.

MUSIC: When I needed a neighbour, were you there   JP275
                Make me a channel of your peace   JP161/MP456
                If you see someone lying in the road   JP95
                (*see also Love*)

31

THEME: *Celebration*

AIM: To help the children appreciate that it is important to celebrate, and that God wants us to enjoy our celebrations.

AIDS: *Wedding photographs.*

LEADER: Is it anyone's birthday today? Next week? Why do we sing "Happy Birthday" to a person on their special day? Yes, because we want to share their happiness.

Has anyone been to a wedding? Here are some photographs of weddings; pass them round and have a look. There are bridesmaids and page boys, flowers and special food . . . all to celebrate.

God likes us to celebrate and share happiness with one another. Jesus went as a guest to a wedding feast and he helped the bride and groom when they had a catering problem.
(*Read the story from John chapter 2.*)

PRAYER FOCUS: *Thanksgiving for so many events, birthdays, weddings, etc. to celebrate together; help to be generous in our sharing so that no one is hurt by being deliberately excluded.*

BIBLE TEXT: *A wedding took place at Cana in Galilee. Jesus' mother was there, and Jesus and his disciples had also been invited to the wedding.*   John 2:1

MUSIC: God is good, we sing and shout it   JP55/MP185
                I will sing, I will sing a song unto the Lord   JP126/MP313
                Give me oil in my lamp, keep me burning   JP50/MP167
                (from verse 2/3)

Cheerfulness

AIM: To show how loving and kind we can be by just being cheerful.

AIDS: *None.*

LEADER: Has anyone here ever been to hospital? No, not to visit but to stay in for treatment.

It is not easy to keep cheerful when you are not feeling very well; and it can be boring.

Here is a story about two boys in hospital and how the wonderful kindness and cheerfulness of one helped the other.

Two boys, strangers to one another but both ten years of age, were moved to the same small, side ward of a general hospital. Simon, placed by the only window, was the fitter and more active, although like Martin, he was confined to bed.

At first Martin was very poorly, unhappy and depressed; but Simon succeeded in cheering him up.

As he gained in strength Martin was daily entertained by his new friend, who brightened each day with vivid descriptions of what he could see from the window alongside his bed. Through the spring and into the early summer Simon told Martin of the daffodils coming out in the park across the street; told him about the children playing on the swings

A cheerful heart is good medicine.
Proverbs 17:22

and roundabout; spoke of the old and young that passed in the street below.

The sad day came when the boys were parted. Simon was sent off for convalescence and Martin asked to be moved to the bed by the window. Sister would not permit it; she gave good reasons but that did not stop Martin from asking again and again. One day a new Sister was put on the ward. Martin seized the opportunity and asked her. He was moved. With eager anticipation Martin looked out of the window. He looked and looked again in stunned disbelief; there was nothing there but a blank brick wall and at its foot a squalid yard with a row of dustbins. For two months Simon had worked hard, hour after hour, to cheer up Martin with his vivid imagination.

That is real friendship; putting yourself out for someone else.

PRAYER
FOCUS:
Thanksgiving for God's love; help to hear and respond to Jesus when he asks us to love one another and realize that means making an effort to be cheerful, for the sake of others.

MUSIC:
If you want joy, real joy, wonderful joy   JP96
I've got that joy, joy, joy, joy   JP121
The joy of the Lord is my strength   JP240

Children's Rights

AIM: To help the children appreciate that they have certain basic rights which are in total agreement with the care Jesus would expect adults to have for all children.

AIDS: *A reader.*

LEADER: You may have heard of the very big war which went on over 50 years ago, called the Second World War. It caused the death of many people, 55 million in all; and very many were injured too.

   After that war a charter or list of grown-up's rights – the things everyone should have – was issued. A few years later another list of children's rights was drawn up; here it is.

CHILD
READER: Children have a right –
   To affection, love and understanding.
   To adequate nutrition and medical care.
   To free education.
   To full opportunity for play and recreation.
   To a name and nationality.
   To special care, if handicapped.
   To be among the first to receive relief in times of disaster.
   To learn to be a useful member of society and to develop individual abilities.
   To be brought up in a spirit of peace and universal-brotherhood.

BIBLE TEXT: *Jesus called a little child and had him stand among them.*
                                                              Matthew 18:2

To enjoy these rights, regardless of race, colour,
     sex, religion, national or social origin.
(*UN Declaration of the Rights of the Child*)

PRAYER   *Our gratitude for the freedom and love that we all enjoy*
FOCUS: *in this country; for those millions of boys and girls in other*
              countries who do not enjoy the rights that we take for
              granted.

MUSIC: Jesus died for all the children   JP132
              In our work and in our play   JP108
              Make me a channel of your peace   JP161/MP456

Christ

AIM: To help the children understand the title "Christ".

AIDS: *Prepared cards each with a title, eg, Mrs, Lord, Doctor, Madam, Reverend, etc. A more decorative one with the word, "Christ"; the leader keeps this one.*

LEADER: (*Distribute the cards among the children.*) Without showing everyone your card would those with cards come out to the front.

We are going to talk about titles, for example what title do you think comes in front of my name on an envelope when someone writes to me? Yes, *Reverend.* (*Card held up.*)

Let's try another one. What title appears before the name of a married woman? Yes, *Mrs.* (*Card help up.*)

What title do we give to a man or woman who helps us get better, when we are ill? (*Doctor card held up.*) (*Continue with other titles, at will.*)

Now what title was given to Jesus of Nazareth? Yes, *the Christ.* (*Leader holds up his card.*)

The word means "annointed", which means rubbed with oil. The Jewish kings and priests were consecrated, that is made special for God's service, by being annointed. People believed that a very special person THE annointed – the Christ – would come. The friends of Jesus believed, and we believe that Jesus was God's special person.

BIBLE TEXT: *"Who do you say I am?" Simon Peter answered, "You are the Christ, the Son of the living God."*

Matthew 16:16

PRAYER FOCUS: *Gratitude for God the Father's love in sending Jesus as the Christ; help to be faithful in our following of the Christ.*

MUSIC: Christ triumphant ever reigning   JP25/MP77
We really want to thank you, Lord   JP268/MP734
Lord Jesus Christ   JP156/MP435
(see also Christ – Human Like Us
Christ – Light of the World)

Christ –
Human Like Us

AIM: To reveal the human nature of Jesus Christ.

AIDS: *Four volunteers to read and hold four large cards with the words ANGRY TIRED HUNGRY UPSET. If possible, a large devotional picture of Jesus for the leader to use.*

LEADER: We have all seen pictures of Jesus, like this one (*hold up the picture*) which shows a lovely person who is wonderful, gentle and perfect. This can give us the wrong impression, because although he was a lovely person he was like us in every way, except he could not sin. (*The four readers have their short readings on the back of their cards which they hold up to view as they read.*)

READER A: ANGRY . . . On reaching Jerusalem, Jesus entered the temple area and began driving out those who were buying and selling there. He overturned the tables of the money changers and the benches of those who were selling doves. Mark 11:15

READER B: TIRED . . . As they sailed, he fell asleep. A storm came down on the lake, so that the boat was swamped . . . his disciples went and woke Jesus. Luke 8:22

READER C: HUNGRY . . . Jesus was led by the Spirit in the desert . . . he ate nothing and was hungry. Luke 4:2

BIBLE TEXT: *Because Jesus himself suffered when he was tempted, he is able to help those who are being tempted.*

Hebrews 2:18

READER D: UPSET . . . When Jesus saw Mary weeping he was deeply moved in spirit and troubled. "Where have you laid his body?" he asked. "Come and see Lord," they replied. Jesus wept. John 11:33

LEADER: We get angry – we get tired – we get hungry – we get upset. Jesus our Saviour was like us; only different in one way, he could not deliberately break one of God's commandments.

Jesus was, and will always be, truly human, just like us – except he cannot hurt God, he cannot sin.

PRAYER FOCUS: *Thankfulness for God's gift of Jesus, our Saviour; help to appreciate that he is really human, like us.*

MUSIC: "Follow me," says Jesus JP46
Lord Jesus Christ JP156/MP435
(See also Christ and Christ – Light of the World)

THEME: *Christ –*
Light of The World

AIM: To make clear an important concept about Jesus which would not be immediately obvious to children.

AIDS: *A hand spotlight or large torch, which gives a good beam of light.*

LEADER: (*Hold and demonstrate the spotlight.*) Have you one of these at home? It's really fun to go outside on a dark evening and see how far the beam of light will reach. (*Be careful not to offend anyone by shining it at them.*)

That reminds me of a true story. A man was flying his single-engine airplane towards a small country airport. It was late in the day, and before he could get the plane into position to land, it got dark and he could not see the hazy field below. He had no lights on his plane and there was no one on duty at the small airstrip. He felt desperate. He did the only thing that he could, he kept circling round and round; but of course it only got darker. This went on for over an hour; he did not know what else to do. The pilot knew that soon when his fuel was used up he would crash to his death.

Then his prayers were answered; someone on the ground heard the plane's engine and guessed what the problem was. This man drove his car up and down on the runway, with his lights full on, to show where the strip was; then he parked at the far end of the runway to guide the plane into a safe landing with his headlights. The stranger saved the life of the pilot.

Christ is the light of our lives; he lights up for us the way that we should go . . . if we are going to be safe in our friendship with God.

PRAYER FOCUS: *Thanksgiving for Jesus, our light and guide; help to follow the way Jesus shows us.*

MUSIC: Colours of Day   JP28
I am a lighthouse   JP87
Jesus bids us shine   JP128
Keep me shining, Lord   JP147
(*see also Christ, and Christ – Human Like Us*)

Christmas (1)

AIM: To bring home the real nature and purpose of Christmas.

AIDS: *A gift-wrapped parcel.*

LEADER: On which two special days in the year would you expect to receive a gift like this (*hold up the gift*)? Yes, on your birthday and at Christmas. Is there anyone here who has a birthday at Christmas time? Christmas gifts and birthday presents get mixed up, don't they?

BIBLE TEXT: *Mary gave birth to a son. And Joseph gave him the name Jesus.* Matthew 1:25

Here's a little story for you.

The first Christmas that little Linda learned to read she was allowed to distribute the family gifts on Christmas morning.

According to their family custom, the one who gave out the presents could open the first parcel. After all the gifts were distributed with loving care Linda kept looking and looking around the tree. Linda's father asked, "What are you looking for, dear?" Linda replied, "I thought Christmas was Jesus' birthday and I was just wondering where his present is. It looks as though everyone forgot him."

It is easy, in all the excitement of Christmas, to forget why the decorations are up, why we are giving gifts, etc. If today was the birthday of one of you here in front of me now, you would be embarrassed, but like it if we now sang "Happy Birthday to you . . ." Let's all do that now for Jesus. "Happy Birthday . . ."

PRAYER FOCUS: *Thank you for birthdays and Christmas; may we never forget that Christmas is a birthday.*

MUSIC: Away in a manger   JP12/MP47
Hark! The herald-angels sing   JP69/MP211
Mary had a little baby   JP164
(*see also Christmas (2)*)

45

Christmas (2)

AIM: To give a different and memorable slant to the message that God gave his Son out of love for all.

AIDS: *In preparation for the service, perhaps in Sunday School, the children who are to read could draw pictures of the animals in the story and have them exhibited while they read. The young readers need to rehearse beforehand.*

LEADER: You know how the shepherds visited the stable on the night that Jesus was born. Well, there is a lovely ancient story that at midnight on that very special night the animals made their own visit to the Saviour Jesus. We now have a poem about this found in some papers by a young friend.

In the barn on Christmas Eve,
After all the people leave,
The animals, in voices low,
Remember Christmas long ago.

FIRST CHILD
READER
(HEN): One small hen, upon her nest,
Softly clucks to all the rest;
"Little chicks, come, gather near
A wondrous story you will hear."

BIBLE TEXT: *Mary wrapped the baby in swaddling clothes and laid him in a manger.* Luke 2:7

READER
(DOVE):

Two white doves, on rafters high,
Coo a quiet lullaby:
"Long ago in manger hay,
The little baby Jesus lay."

Three wise men from far away
Came to visit him one day,
"For he was born," the doves recall,
"To be the greatest king of all."

READER
(HORSE):

Four brown horses in their stalls,
Snug within the stable walls,
Tell of his birth: "T'was long foretold
By chosen men in days of old."

READER
(DONKEY):

Five grey donkeys speak with pride,
Remembering one who gave a ride:
"Our brother donkey went with them
From Nazareth to Bethlehem."

READER
(CALF):

Six spotted calves now nibble hay
Like that on which the baby lay.
"They put him in a manger bed
So he could rest his sleepy head."

READER
(GOAT):

Seven goats, all black and white,
Describe the sky that holy night:
"A star appeared at early morn
To mark the place where he was born."

READER (KITTEN):	Eight nestling kittens lick their fur. They nod their heads and softly purr: "And he was wrapped in swaddling clothes To keep him warm from head to toes."
READER (SHEEP):	Nine woolly sheep, down from the hill, On Christmas Eve remember still: "Shepherds heard the angels sing Praises to the newborn king."
READER (LAMB):	Ten soft lambs say Jesus' name; "He was the Lamb of God who came. He was the greatest gift of love, Sent from his Father, God, above."
READER (PUPPY):	Eleven puppies listen well, In hopes that they, in turn, can tell The Christmas story another year For all the animals to hear.
LEADER:	Twelve chimes ring out from far away, The lovely bells of Christmas Day. And every beast bows low its head For one small babe in a manger bed.

(Author unknown)

PRAYER
FOCUS:
Thanksgiving for the lovely time we have at Christmas; all creation, animal and birds give thanks, with us, for the birth of Jesus our Saviour.

MUSIC: Jesus Christ the Lord is born   JP131
The first nowell   JP238/MP644
(*Any suitable carol. See also Christmas (1)*)

Citizenship

AIM: To introduce children to the idea that being good members of society is what Christ asks of us.

AIDS: *A selection of foreign coins. A reader.*

LEADER: I have just been round and given (lent) you a coin each; please have a good look at that coin. Can you work out which country it comes from; does it have a date?

How many of you have a coin with a person's face or head on it? Can anyone tell me the meaning of the word, "tax"? Yes, that's right. It is a sum of money that grown-ups pay to the Government to help pay for the service they provide for the people of the country. Let us now listen to a reading of the story of how some men tried to catch Jesus out.

READER: The chief priests and the scribes kept a watch on Jesus to try and catch him out. They were looking for an opportunity to report him to the Roman governor. These men put a trick question to Jesus, "Master", they said, "we know that you have the right teaching, and you are not afraid of anyone. Tell us, is it right that we should pay taxes to Caesar, the Roman Emperor, or not?"

Jesus saw their trap. "Show me a Roman coin," he said.

"Whose head and whose name is on this coin?"

Give to Caesar what is Caesar's, and to God what is God's.
Matthew 22:21

"Caesar's," they said.

"Then," he said to them, "you should pay back to Caesar what belongs to Caesar. And to God what belongs to God." They all marvelled at his answer, and said no more.

LEADER: Jesus told the people to pay their taxes. All his friends and followers should do the same because that is one way in which we can be good Christians. It is called 'citizenship'; playing a proper and fair part in the community.

PRAYER FOCUS: *Thankfulness for the peaceful and fair society in which we live; help to play a bigger and bigger part in society as we grow older.*

MUSIC: We shall overcome (*verses 1, 2 & 4*)   JP270
We really want to thank you, Lord   JP268/MP734
When I needed a neighbour   JP275
When Israel was in Egypt's land   JP276

The Commandments

AIM: To help the children appreciate the importance and need for the commandments of God.

AIDS: *As many books or manuals of instruction for new appliances as possible, with the target of one per child. However only one such book is really necessary for the leader. A reader.*

LEADER: When we bought, in our home, a new (washing machine/carpet sweeper/dishwasher, etc) we received this book of instructions at the same time. If I have given you one like this have a good look at it now.

You will see that it tells you how to wire the appliance with the correct plug. It then tells you how to use it correctly in order to get the best out of your appliance. The manual also tells you what NOT to do, otherwise you will damage the appliance.

Now put the books down and think. We believe that God has made human beings. Has God given us a kind of list of instructions to follow in order to live a complete life?

Yes, you are right. It is found in the Bible. But where precisely? It is the Ten Commandments. Here they are –

BIBLE TEXT: *Fear God and keep his commandments,*
for this is the whole duty of man.
Ecclesiastes 12:13

READER: I am your God . . .
You must worship no other gods;
You must not make any images to worship;
You must not use my name in wrong ways;
You must do no work on the Sabbath;
You must never despise your father and mother;
You must not kill;
You must not commit adultery;
You must not steal;
You must not bear false witness against anybody;
You must not covet anybody else's family property.
(*A. Dale's Winding Quest*)

Keep these, Jesus told a rich young man (*Luke 18:18*)
and you will inherit life with God; which is the
purpose of human life.

PRAYER
FOCUS: *Thankfulness for God's guidance and plan for each of us;*
help to keep God's commandments.

MUSIC: Father, lead me day by day   JP43
The best book to read is the Bible   JP234
Seek ye first the Kingdom of God   JP215/MP590

THEME: *Community*

AIM: To help the children appreciate that in a Christian community, like the local church or parish, we all need one another and Christ is at the centre of the community.

AIDS: *One house brick, one cauliflower (or cabbage), one branch from a rose bush. A reader.*

LEADER: Let us first listen to what Jesus said to his friends at the last meal he had with them before he died.

READER: I am the real vine and my Father is the farmer who looks after it. He cuts off every unfruitful branch, and he prunes every fruitful branch to make it more fruitful still. A branch dies if it gets broken off the vine – no fruit can grow on it . . . I am the vine, you are the branches. (*John 15, Alan Dale version*)

LEADER: Can anyone tell me what a vine is? What grows on a vine? Yes, grapes. You can see them in this country but they are not as common as where Jesus lived in his time.

I have three objects here; a house brick, a cauliflower and a branch from a rose bush. The question I want you to think about is this. Which of these three is the odd one out; which one, in one particular way, does not fit. The clue is in the reading we have just heard.

No, it is not the house brick because it has not

BIBLE TEXT: *I am the vine; you are the branches.*
John 15:5

grown; nor is it the rose branch because it has thorns.

Yes, the odd one out is the cauliflower because it grows on its own. It is complete on its own. The brick is part of a wall and the rose-branch is part of a bush.

That is the same, of course, as a vine. Jesus says the Christian community is like a vine or a rose bush. He is the stem, from which we the branches get our life and strength. We need Christ and we need one another.

PRAYER
FOCUS: *Thank God for Jesus as the source of our life and strength as Christians; help to understand and appreciate that in a Christian community we need one another.*

MUSIC: Bind us together, Lord   JP17/MP54
For I'm building a people of power   JP47/MP151
All over the world the Spirit is moving   JP5/MP18

Complaining

AIM: To show how grateful we should be for everything –
       we have no cause to complain.

AIDS: *A reader.*

LEADER: Do you ever complain? God does not like us to
          complain because he has given us so much to be
          grateful for. Some time ago I came across the
          following poem in a book; no one knows who wrote
          it but it has a good lesson to teach.

READER: Today upon a bus, I saw a lovely maid
              with golden hair;
          I envied her, she had such joy, and
              wished I were so fair.
          When suddenly she rose to leave, I saw
              her hobble down the aisle;
          She had one foot and wore a crutch, but
              as she passed, a smile.
          Oh, God, forgive me when I whine;
          I have two feet, the world is mine.

          And then I stopped to buy some sweets.
              The lad who sold them had
          Such charm, I talked with him – he said
              to me;
          "It's nice to talk with folks like you.
          You see," he said, "I'm blind."
          Oh, God, forgive me when I whine;
          I have two eyes, the world is mine.

BIBLE TEXT: *Do everything without complaining or arguing . . . so that you may become children of God.* Philippians 2:14

Then, walking down the street, I saw
    a child with eyes of blue.
He stood and watched the others play;
It seemed he knew not what to do.
I stopped for a moment, then I said:
"Why don't you join the others, dear?"
He looked ahead without a word, and then
I knew he could not hear.
Oh, God, forgive me when I whine;
I have two ears, the world is mine.

With feet to take me where I'd go,
With eyes to see the sunset's glow,
With ears to hear what I would know,
Oh, God, forgive me when I whine;
I'm blessed indeed. The world is mine.

PRAYER
FOCUS: *Thanksgiving for feet and eyes and hearing; help to be always grateful and never complaining.*

MUSIC: Give me oil in my lamp   JP50/MP167
God is good, we sing and shout it   JP55/MP185
Thank you for ev'ry new good morning   JP230
Thank you, Lord, for this fine day   JP232

THEME: *Conscience*

AIM: To encourage the children to think about "conscience" and deepen their understanding.

AIDS: *A reader.*

LEADER: Have you ever done something which you know is wrong, like taking money from your mother's purse, or telling an untrue story about someone; and afterwards you feel very bad about it? The little voice inside that says to you, "That was wrong, you should not have done it"; that little voice is called your conscience. Here is how an Indian Christian described conscience.

READER: "Oh, yes," said the Indian, "I know what conscience is. It is a little three-cornered thing in here," he laid his hand on his heart, "that stands still when I am good; but when I am bad, it turns round, and the corners hurt very much. But if I keep on doing wrong, by-and-by the corners wear off and it doesn't hurt any more." (*J. Ellis*)

LEADER: We should notice the last point; if we keep ignoring the warnings we get from our conscience we will lose any hope of being good.

BIBLE TEXT: *The goal of this command is love, which comes from a pure heart and a good conscience and a sincere faith.*

                                                                1 Timothy 1:5

PRAYER   *Thankfulness to God for giving each of us a conscience to*
FOCUS: *warn us of when we have done wrong; help to take care of*
              our precious gift, so that we can become better people.

MUSIC: Be still and know that I am God   JP22/MP48
              Cleanse me from my sin, Lord   JP27/MP82
              Amazing Grace (*verses 1, 2 & 3*)   JP8/MP31

Contentment

AIM: To help the children be content with themselves as they are.

AIDS: *None.*

LEADER: Today I have a story for you to illustrate the theme. Once there was a snake that was greatly displeased at the horror he seemed to excite in everyone. He was conscious of his innocence and could not understand why everybody ran away from him, or, if they stopped, threw sticks and stones at him with cries of anger. He concluded that it was merely on account of his personal appearance, and made up his mind to change that. Therefore placing his tail in his mouth and forming himself into a perfect circle, he stiffened himself so that he appeared perfectly wooden. In this condition he was found by some children, who pounced upon him with eagerness, crying out, "Oh, what a pretty green hoop." Taking a stick, they began to trundle the hoop along, giving it a smart blow with the stick at every turn. The poor snake endured this torture as long as he could, and then took an opportunity to roll off among the bushes and speedily assumed his proper shape and slipped into a hole.

"I have learned," said the snake, "that however unfortunate one thinks one's lot is, nothing is to

BIBLE TEXT: *I have learned to be content, whatever the circumstances.*
Philippians 4:11

be gained from pretending to be something or
someone else."   (*A. R. Wells*)

We are as God has made us; rather than worry
about our height or weight or hair colouring or
whatever it might be, let us accept ourselves as we
are and get on with trying to live lovingly as
Christians.

PRAYER
FOCUS:
*Thankfulness for good health and well-being; help to
always accept ourselves as we are.*

MUSIC:
If I were a butterfly   JP94
Happiness is to know the Saviour   JP70
It's a happy day   JP118
(*see also Happiness*)

Creation

AIM: To link children's observation of nature today with the creative action of God and his concern for his creation.

AIDS: *Several jam jar with garden snails.*

LEADER: (*Hand the jam jars round for the children to look at.*) Most children enjoy watching snails; they are interesting to watch and can be found in most gardens. If you are quiet they come out of their shells and move around with their little antennae coming out to sense what is going on.

Did you know that there are about 50,000 different kinds of snail? Also they are very unusual animals that can be found on the land, in the sea and also in freshwater. Isn't God wonderful? Who could imagine so many different types of snail?

In the reading we have just heard from Genesis, the first book of the Bible, it says, "Let the land produce living creatures that move along the ground"; the snail was created by God, in 50,000 different types. Amazing. It is the same with other creatures God created; he did not just create bats, there are 20,000 different kinds of bat; and you know there are thousands of different types of fish . . . and so it goes on.

When you watch a snail, or a worm or some other creature God has made think how wonderful God is

BIBLE TEXT: *And God said, "Let the land produce living creatures according to their kinds: livestock, creatures that move along the ground . . ." and God saw that it was good.*

Genesis 1:24

to have created such an incredible variety of interesting inhabitants for our world.

The next thing to realize is how we must take care of God's creation and not kill or destroy any creature without very good reason.

Now I will have the jam jars back so that I can return the snails to the garden where they come from.

PRAYER
FOCUS:
Thanksgiving for the wonders of God's creation; help to care for this world entrusted to us by God.

MUSIC:
All things bright and beautiful   JP6/MP23
For the beauty of the earth   JP48/MP152
God, whose farm is all creation   JP61
He made the stars to shine   JP76
Who put the colours in the rainbow   JP288
(*see also Taking Care of our World, and Nature*)

THEME: *Dignity*

AIM: To help the children appreciate that although we all look different, etc. we are all imbued with the same spirit; created in the likeness of God.

AIDS: *Five or six candles of different sizes, shapes and colours (tall, short, thin, red, white, etc). Arrange these where they can be clearly seen.*

LEADER: (*Light the candles.*) Look carefully at these different candles as I light them. Each one is different, there's a (*insert a description of what you have on display*) . . . Now look at the flame. Each candle has a flame and each flame is exactly the same . . . all the different candles share the same flame.

Think about it. There is no difference in the size or quality of the flame, regardless of the shape and size of the candles.

Now think of people. We are all different to look at; there are tall people and short people; fat people and thin people; white people and black people, etc. BUT the spirit within, God's presence, is the same.

The Book of Genesis tells us that we are made in the image of God . . . and so we are; on the inside where our power to love is.

We each have a wonderful dignity from this likeness to God; and we must respect that dignity in everyone.

BIBLE TEXT: *So God created man in his own image,*
              in the image of God he created him.
                                        Genesis 1:27

PRAYER   *Gratitude for my uniqueness; that we may remember our*
FOCUS: *own personal dignity and, with God's help, respect it in*
              everyone else.

MUSIC: He gave me eyes so I could see   JP74
              Two little eyes to look to God   JP262
              If I were a butterfly   JP94
              Whether you're one or whether you're two   JP284
              (*see also Special Person*)

Do Not Fear

AIM: To reassure the children that when they are frightened of anything God is close as a loving Father. He does not want them to fear.

AIDS: *Pieces of white card or paper cut in the shape of a sparrow.*

LEADER: Hands up anyone who is afraid of the dark.
Hands up anyone who is afraid of spiders.
Hands up anyone who is afraid of a teacher at school.

Many people are afraid; some are afraid of heights; some of open spaces; some of tunnels and so on. But God does not want us to be afraid.

Each time God sent a message to people, the message started with the words, "Do not be afraid." For example,

> When God appears to Isaac in the Book of Genesis
>
> When the angel Gabriel took God's message to Zachariah.
>
> When Gabriel took God's message to Mary.

God really does not want us to be afraid. Through the Old Testament prophet, Isaiah, God says to us: "Do not be afraid, for I have redeemed you; I have called you by name, you are mine." (*Isaiah 43:1*)

And Jesus says we are more precious than many sparrows, and the Father knows about each one of them.

BIBLE TEXT: *Are not two sparrows sold for a penny? Yet not one of them will fall to the ground apart from the will of your Father . . . So don't be afraid; you are worth more than many sparrows.* Matthew 10:29

On the sparrow-shape you have received write down one thing that you are frightened of: then a little prayer, like "God help me not to be afraid" or "Lord may I trust you."

PRAYER FOCUS: *Thankfulness for God's protecting love; help to face up to any fears and to trust in God's loving care.*

MUSIC: The King of love my shepherd is   JP241/MP649
Be still and know that I am God   JP22/MP48
Put you hand in the hand   JP206
Father, I place into your hands   JP42/MP133
(*see also* Trust in God)

Duty to Parents

AIM: To help children appreciate the meaning of the commandment.

AIDS: *If possible, a girl with long hair and a hair-brush; and a volunteer to brush the girl's hair. A reader.*

LEADER: I have asked (name) to sit here and (name) to carefully brush her hair for her.

Do you know that at the beginning of this century, around about 1910, it was usual for girls to brush their mother's hair for them, and help them to dress. Listen to this from the childhood of the famous writer, Elizabeth Goudge.

READER: Mothers get dressed so quickly in these days that their offspring cannot get much fun out of helping them to do it. A zip-fastener, if it does not stick, is switched up the back in a moment, but hooking your mother up the back when heaven alone knew how many hooks and eyes you had to manipulate was a work of art, and required much practice and heavy breathing on the part of the child, and much patience on the part of the mother. Hair had to be brushed with a hundred strokes a day. When it was up it was coiled on top of the head like a crown, and when down it was a matter of pride if a child could boast that its mother could sit on her hair. My mother could and it was a joke between us that she

Honour your father and your mother.
Exodus 20:12

could have emulated Lady Godiva. Her hair was brown with golden lights and so full of electricity that on frosty days it sprang about her head like snakes when it was brushed. (*The Joy of the Snow*, Spire Books)

LEADER: There were many other things, in those days, that children were expected to do to help their parents. (*Adapt as necessary.*) My grandmother used to take three days to do her weekly washing and I was expected to help by turning the handle of the mangle, and many other tasks.

We have a duty to help our parents. The word "honour" in the commandment means to respect them; we cannot give them respect and just sit around and not offer to help in whatever way we can. When asked to help we must not moan, but be generous in our love and respect.

PRAYER
FOCUS:
Thank God for our parents and a comfortable home; ask for help to be respectful and helpful to them at all times.

MUSIC: Bind us together Lord   JP17/MP54
Father, I place into your hands   JP42/MP133
He's got the whole wide world   JP78/MP225
(*see also Family*)

AIM: To relate and draw out from the chocolate Easter egg the real meaning of Easter.

AIDS: *One hard-boiled egg; one round smooth stone or pebble (as like an egg in appearance as possible); one chocolate Easter egg; and one pocket calculator.*

LEADER: (*Address the children.*) Why do you have chocolate eggs given to you as a present today?

(*Answers vary; even if an older child makes some reply similar to the one intended, proceed for the sake of them all.*)

Can you imagine for a moment a space ship landing from outer space? The landing site it chooses is a wide, pebbly beach. After a few minutes a hatch opens and out steps a strange-looking little space traveller. He looks around at the scenery – there's no one in sight. Bending down he picks up one of the round/oval stones. (*Imitate action with the aid.*) He weights it in his hands, then tests it with a little calculator-like box in his left hand. It's smooth, cold and lifeless. He looks around at a beach full of the same lifeless stones.

Our space traveller walks up the beach to a bank of grass. After inspecting that he sees in the distance a farm-house with barns and outhouses. He walks cautiously towards the buildings. Half-way there he almost steps on a cluster of brown,

Very early in the morning of the first day of the week the women went to the tomb, just as the sun was rising.

Mark 16:2

oval, stone-like objects. "More stones," he thinks; but when he picks one up it's warm. He runs his little machine over it and finds, to his amazement, that there are signs of life inside; inside what looks like a dead stone. (*Hold up the hard-boiled egg and say, "Eggs really do look and feel like stones".*)

As the alien holds the egg in his hand it cracks – once – twice – three times and, as he watches, a little chick pushes his head out into the world.

You can imagine the surprise of the space traveller; new life from what looked like a dead stone. It is a perfect example of what happened on the first Easter morning. The stone, behind which Jesus had been buried, looked cold and dead, but suddenly new life burst out of it – Jesus was alive.

When you break open – if you haven't done that already – your Easter egg remember what it stands for.

PRAYER FOCUS: *Thankfulness for the Resurrection of Jesus; help to understand the real meaning of Easter.*

MUSIC: He is Lord   JP75/MP220
Morning has broken   JP166/MP467
This is the day   JP255/MP691
(*see also Easter (2)*)d

.71

Easter (2)

AIM: To help the children understand the importance of Easter and the belief that Jesus has risen.

AIDS: *Letters A,L,I,V,E on a separate sheet. One child for each letter.*

LEADER: A little boy was taken to church on Easter morning by his grandmother. When he got home his mother asked about the service. He said, "I understand about Christ, but not about the roses." "What roses?" asked his mother. "The minister" said the boy, "kept saying that Jesus was a rose." "No," said his grandmother, who had been listening, "the minister said Jesus rose from the dead."

Have you ever heard this little rhyme?

> One, two, three, four, five,
> Jesus is alive,
> Six, seven, eight, nine, ten,
> He will come again.

Let's all say it together . . .

Now this time, when we say, one, two, three, four, five the boys and girls with the letters will hold them up one at a time for us all to see.

ALIVE that means that Jesus is with us; he is not a dead person of history, like Henry VIII, but a living person who can be with us at any time.

72

BIBLE TEXT: *After his sufferings Jesus showed himself and gave many*
convincing proofs that he was alive. Acts 1:3

PRAYER
FOCUS: *Thankfulness for the strong belief we have that Jesus came*
back from the dead to be with us always; help to turn to our
friend in prayer every day.

MUSIC Led like a lamb JP151/MP402
Now the green blade riseth JP174
Alleluia, Alleluia, give thanks to the risen Lord JP3/MP30
(see also Easter (1) and Risen Lord)

73

Facing up to Failure

To encourage the children not to give up when faced with difficulties.

The words of the song in the hands of the children so that they can join in.

Do you know the song "Nellie the Elephant"? Let's sing it together:

> Nellie the elephant packed her trunk
> And said "good-bye" to the circus
> Off she went with a trumpety trump,
> Trump, trump, trump. Etc.

Nellie ran away from the circus. Many people are not happy about how animals are made to perform in a circus; but Nellie made up her own mind and ran away. Have you ever thought of running away from home?

When we feel a failure, or we feel that our family doesn't love us any more, or we are not understood, the temptation comes to run away. Don't ever do that, for lots of reasons: it could be very dangerous for you; you would give great pain and distress to those who love you; and it is never the answer to a problem to run away from it.

When Jesus knew that he would have to suffer the death of the cross he cried out to his Father for help (*Matthew 26:39*) and he could have run away in

BIBLE TEXT: *Consider it pure joy whenever you face trials of many kinds, because you know that the testing of your faith develops perseverance.* James 1:2

---

the darkness; but he did not do that, he resisted the temptation and faced up to the suffering.

PRAYER
FOCUS: *Thanksgiving for our home and family; help to have the courage to face up to a feeling of failure and place all trust in the love of God our Father.*

MUSIC: Father, I place into your hands   JP42/MP133
Father, lead me day by day   JP43
One more step along the world I go   JP188

Faith

AIM: To develop the children's understanding of faith and its growth.

AIDS: *A packet of seeds and some card or paper cut into tree shapes. A card with the words, "Let my faith grow this big" for the young ones to copy.*

BIBLE TEXT: *It is like a mustard seed, which is the smallest seed you*
              plant in the ground. Yet when planted, it grows and
              becomes the largest of all garden plants.   Mark 4:31

LEADER: If you hold out your hand I will come round and put
          a few small seeds in it. Now see how small they are.
          Jesus tells us that seeds which are smaller than what
          you have in your hand, mustard seeds, grow into
          trees big enough for the birds to come and perch in
          them.

          It seems impossible, doesn't it, that a dried-up
          dead-looking seed, like the ones we have here,
          should ever grow at all; let alone into something
          big. That is the wonder of God's creation.

          God gives us the gift of faith. It is very small
          when we receive it – like the seed. Now we can
          throw the seed away or we can plant it and water it
          and watch over it while it grows. The same is true of
          faith. We can throw the gift away, or we can take
          care of it and watch over it while it grows. If we
          want our faith to grow God will help us.

          Now, on the "tree shapes" I want you to write
          this little prayer: Let my faith grow this big.

PRAYER   *Thankfulness for the gift of faith; help to pray and work at*
FOCUS: *the care of the gift, so that it grows into a big tree.*

MUSIC: Be still and know that I am God   JP22/MP48
          Father we adore you   JP45/MP139
          My faith is like a staff of oak   JP168

77

Family

AIM: To encourage the children to think of their families as communities in which they have an active part.

AIDS: *Pictures of sporting teams, e.g. football; and pictures of an orchestra or band.*

LEADER: I am going to pass round some team pictures and also some pictures of an orchestra (band). When you have all looked at them perhaps you could tell me what you think they have in common, what they share. Yes, they are both made up of people, but what I was hoping you would say is that they can only succeed as a team or an orchestra if they work together. That is where they are both the same as a family. A family was meant by God to be a team. Each member of the family helping one another.

Did you ever think about Jesus being a member of a family? Could you imagine Jesus sitting back and lazily doing nothing to help in the home? If parents help children and children help parents, there will be a team spirit; a community of love and a happy family.

PRAYER
FOCUS: *Gratitude to God for our families; help to be better at helping and building a team spirit in the home.*

BIBLE TEXT: *Then Jesus went down to Nazareth with Mary and Joseph and was obedient to them.* Luke 2:51

MUSIC: Bind us together, Lord   JP17/MP54
Father, I place into your hands   JP42/MP133
He's got the whole wide world in his hands   JP78/MP225
(*see also Duty to Parents*)

Father's Day (1)

AIM: Father's Day may be of secular origin but it is an opportunity for the children to remember the respect due to parents.

AIDS: *None.*

LEADER: You may think that it is easy to be a mum or a dad. Actually it is quite hard. There is so much to do, so much to think about, plan and find money for. I hope this story will remind you about praying for your parents.

One day a little boy of five was left alone with his father at bedtime. It had never happened before. After his bath and some fun together the little boy got his pyjamas on. His father was just about to lift him into bed when the little boy said, "Daddy, I have to say my prayers first." He knelt down beside his bed, joined his hands and prayed, "Now I lay me down to sleep, I pray the Lord my soul to keep . . ." When he had finished his usual prayers he looked at his Dad, and carried on praying, 'Dear God, make me a great big good man, like my daddy. Amen."

In a moment he was in bed, and in five minutes, he was asleep. And then his father knelt by his son's bed and prayed, "Dear Lord, make me a great big good man, like my boy thinks I am."

BIBLE TEXT: *Then Jesus went down to Nazareth with Mary and Joseph and was obedient to them.*   Luke 2:51

The very best present you could ever give your mother or your father is to pray for them; if possible every day.

PRAYER
FOCUS: *Gratitude for mothers and fathers; help for our fathers that they may all be great big good men.*

MUSIC: Think of a world without any flowers   JP254
               Bind us together, Lord   JP17/MP54
               Have you seen the pussy cat?   JP72
               (*see also Father's Day (2)*)

Father's Day (2)

AIM: To remind the children to show their appreciation of their parents by respecting them and praying for them.

AIDS: *A broken toy.*

LEADER: When you break a toy (*hold it to view*) what do you do? Yes, you ask your dad if he will mend it for you. Sometimes he can; he gets out his tools and makes the repair: and off you go. You forget about dad until the next time you need him. We only think about our dads when we need them, and when we need them we expect their whole attention.

That is exactly the way lots of people treat God; only when they need him to mend something or someone do they think of God. Is it surprising that we call God "Father" because he makes us; and, like our dad, he "mends" us when we need it.

We expect God, our loving, heavenly Father to be there when we need him; and our own dad to be around when we need him. We should be very grateful for all that both do for us.

PRAYER
FOCUS: *Thanksgiving for God's fatherly care of us and gratitude for the care our dads take of us; help to show both how we appreciate their love.*

BIBLE TEXT: *Honour your father and your mother*
as the Lord your God has commanded you.
Deuteronomy 5:16

MUSIC: Father, I place into your hands   JP42/MP133
For the beauty of the earth   JP48/MP152
(*see also Father's Day (1)*)

THEME: *Feeding the Hungry*

AIM: For the children to appreciate that Christ expects us to feed the hungry, just as he did.

AIDS: *Five bread-shaped and two fish-shaped cut-outs. A reader.*

LEADER: I have here five bread shapes and two fish shapes (*give these out, one between two or by some fair distribution system*). Can anyone tell me why I have only given out five bread shapes and two fish shapes? Yes because that is what Jesus had to share between the crowd. How big was the crowd of people?
(*Tell the story, if it has not already been read out; or the following can be read.*)

READER: There is a legend about the boy who gave up his five barley loaves and two small fish so that Christ could feed the multitude. It tells how the boy hurried home, after all the fragments had been gathered, and told his mother about the exciting incident.

With eyes still big with wonder, he told her how his five little barley cakes and two dried fish had multiplied in the Saviour's hand until there was enough to satisfy 5,000 hungry people. And then, with a wistful look, he added, "I wonder, Mother, whether it would be that way with everything you gave him."

BIBLE TEXT: *They do not need to go away. You give them something to eat.* Matthew 14:16

LEADER: Now, I would like those who have the bread and fish cut-outs, with the help of those near them, to write or draw on them ONE way that you could help a needy person.

PRAYER FOCUS: *Thankfulness for the food that we enjoy every day; the Lord's help to be generous in sharing what we have with the needy of our world.*

MUSIC: When I needed a neighbour JP275
A boy gave to Jesus five loaves and two fish JP1
Make me a servant JP162
(*see also Helping the Needy*)

THEME: *Forgiveness*

AIM: To help the children understand that there is no limit to the times that Christ expects us to forgive others.

AIDS: *A roll of paper – a spare roll of wallpaper perhaps – with the word "Forgive" written seven times, one below the other, so that the word is revealed again and again as the paper is unrolled. After the seventh "Forgive" write the words "without end".*

LEADER: It is not easy to forgive someone when they have hurt you. Jesus told his friends that they must try hard to forgive. (*Unroll the paper and reveal the word FORGIVE*)

Peter thought that he was being generous when he said, "Shall I forgive seven times?" (*Unroll paper to show the seven "forgives".*)

No, said Jesus, not seven, but seventy-seven times. That means without end . . . go on and on forgiving (*Let the paper unroll in front of the children.*)

PRAYER FOCUS: *Thanks to God for his willingness to forgive us, when we are prepared to forgive others; help to be ready to forgive whatever hurt we feel.*

BIBLE TEXT: *Peter came to Jesus and asked, "Lord, how many times shall I forgive my brother . . . up to seven times?" Jesus answered, "I tell you, not seven times, but seventy-seven times."*   Matthew 18:22

MUSIC:

God forgave my sin in Jesus' name   JP54/MP181
Cleanse me from my sin, Lord   JP27/MP82
Spirit of the living God   JP222/MP612

Free Will

AIM:
To help the children appreciate that God our Father leaves us with a great deal of freedom, to love him or reject him; we are not puppets.

AIDS:
A puppet: a stringed puppet is most suitable but a glove puppet can be used with adaptations. (The leader does not need to be adept at manipulating the puppet.)

LEADER:
(*Demonstrate the puppet.*) When I pull this string his/her arm moves; and look what happens when I pull both of these strings.

When we see puppet shows the person pulling the strings is usually out of sight. The puppet walks, dances and performs when the hidden person pulls the right strings.

Some people think God should be like that; they think God should so control our lives that he is totally in charge. You will sometimes hear people say, "Why did God allow this to happen or that to happen?"

We are not puppets; God gave us free will. God decided to do that, to take that risk, because he wants us to freely choose to love him, freely choose to serve him. A puppet cannot love or serve. The trouble is that not everyone, as you know, uses their free will in the right way; many choose not to love God and not to serve him. God risked that

BIBLE TEXT: *Lord, you are our Father,*
We are the clay, you are the potter
We are the work of your hand.

Isaiah 64:8

when he made us free persons and not robots or puppets.

PRAYER
FOCUS:

Thanksgiving for our great gift of freedom; help to use our freedom to love and serve God.

MUSIC:

Abba, Father, let me be   JP2/MP3
All over the world the Spirit is moving   JP5/MP18
I want to live for Jesus ev'ry day   JP122
Father, lead me day by day   JP43

Gentleness

AIM: To help teach the importance and power of gentleness.

AIDS: *The following little story can be played out with three characters; the sun, the wind and a man with an overcoat. The sun and wind may have masks or carry symbols denoting who they are.*

LEADER: The wind and sun, so the fable goes, once had a quarrel. The wind boasted that he was much stronger than the sun. He said, "You are too meek and gentle. I'll show you what power I have, and how much stronger I am than you. See that old man over there, with a big coat on? You see how I get him to take it off; I can do it much quicker than you can."

"All right," said the sun, "we'll see." So the sun went behind a cloud, but left a little hole so that he could peep through and see what the wind did. The wind blew and blew as hard as he could, causing a terrible storm, but the harder he blew, the tighter the man wrapped his coat around him. In the end the poor old wind had to become calm and give in.

Then it was the sun's turn. He came out from behind the cloud and smiled with gentle sunshine on the old man. After a little while the old man began to mop his brow, then he pulled his coat off. So the gentle sun beat the fierce wind.

BIBLE TEXT: *Come to me, all you who are weary and burdened, and I will give you rest. Take my yoke upon you and learn from me, for I am gentle and humble of heart.*

Matthew 11:29

PRAYER FOCUS: *Jesus described himself as gentle of heart; we pray to be more Christ-like in our gentleness and kindness.*

MUSIC: God is good, we sing and shout it   JP55/MP185
God who made the earth   JP63
Jesus I will come with you   JP138
Jesus' love is very wonderful   JP139

THEME: *Gifts and Talents*

AIM: To encourage the children to seek and develop their gifts and talents; and appreciate their importance.

AIDS: *Three boxes with slits in the lids. Secretly put a large denomination bank note (10) in the first box (numbered one) and secretly put another bank note (5) in the second box (numbered two). The third box, also numbered, contains nothing.*

           A quantity of play money, or if necessary real money. Chose three children to act the part of the three servants. Give the first the equivalent to what is already in box one; the second receives the same value as already secretly hidden in box two; the third child receives one note or coin. A reader.

LEADER: We are going to read now one of the stories that Jesus told. While we read it out three "servants" will put their money in the boxes.

READER: Story of the Talents Matthew 25:14–30 (*Read text*.)

LEADER: When the master returned he rewarded his servants; let us open our boxes. See how the money in the first box has doubled in value; and the same in the second box. Sadly the third box has not increased in value.

           Jesus wants us to use our gifts and talents so that they will grow. (*Talk with the children about their gifts and talents – being able to swim, a fast runner or jumper, playing a musical instrument, make people laugh, etc.*)

BIBLE TEXT: *Well done, good and faithful servant. You have been faithful with a few things; I will put you in charge of many things. Come and share in your Master's happiness.*

Matthew 25:23

PRAYER FOCUS: *Thanksgiving for the gifts we have and have yet to discover; help to find out more about ourselves and to use the talents we have in the service of others.*

MUSIC: He gave me eyes so I could see   JP74
Thank you for ev'ry new good morning   JP230
If I were a butterfly   JP94

THEME: *God of Surprises*

AIM: To help the children appreciate that our God is a God of surprises – sometimes nice ones, but not always so.

AIDS: *Three shoe boxes of the same size; each wrapped identically in gift paper or Christmas paper. One box should be empty, containing just screwed-up newspaper or packaging. The second box should have packaging and a small box in the middle with something "precious" looking, like a "diamond" ring, etc. The third box should simply contain a shoe.*

LEADER: It is exciting to receive a birthday or Christmas present. (*Produce the boxes.*) What do you think you would find in these gift boxes? Will they all have the same surprise present inside?

(*Children draw lots beforehand to decide who will be the three to open the gifts. To the first child.*) Please unwrap your box. Now before you open the lid of the box, what do you think you will find inside? Now look to see what you have.

(*The same is repeated with the remaining two gifts.*)

It was a surprise to find the shoe, wasn't it? God is like that. He is full of surprises. Lovely things happen when we least expect it; sadly sometimes other surprises cause us to be unhappy, for example when someone dies suddenly. But we believe everything is in God's hands and he knows

BIBLE TEXT: *You do not know on what day your Lord will come.*
Matthew 24:42

what he is doing. Even sad surprises can bring about good in the end.

PRAYER
FOCUS:

Thankfulness for a loving Father who cares for us and surprises us with joy sometimes; may he help us when the surprises are sad ones.

MUSIC:

Abba, Father, let me be   JP2/MP3
Be still and know that I am God   JP22/MP48
O Lord my God! When I in awe-some wonder
   JP179/MP506

THEME: *Good Example*

AIM: To help the children appreciate the importance of
          the good example they have received and the good
          example they can give to others.

AIDS: *Cardboard cut-outs or patterns; these could be of a lighted
          candle (to make a link with the Bible text) or of assorted
          animals, plants, trees, etc. Place these on a table apart
          from children. Paper and pencils.*

LEADER: I am going to give out paper and pencils and you
          must get up and go over to the table to choose an
          outline or pattern to draw round. (*When most of the
          children have finished this.*) Now, let us think about
          what you have done. You went and chose a shape;
          now you have a drawing of what you chose. You
          have given shape to an animal, tree or plant. Who
          has given shape to your life? What do I mean? I
          mean who has helped you to be the sort of person
          that you are? Your parents? Your grandparents?
          Your teachers? Who do you think has shown you
          how to be kind or thoughtful? (*Accept suggestions*).
          We call that "good example". There might be
          someone at your school who gives a bad example by
          the way they behave.
              We should model our lives on Jesus, and on those
          who have tried and are trying to live the way Jesus
          asks us to live.

BIBLE TEXT: *Let your light shine before men, that they may see your good deeds and praise your Father in heaven.*

Matthew 5:16

PRAYER
FOCUS
Thanksgiving to the Father for the gift of his son as our model and pattern; help to become more like Jesus and to follow the example of people who try to live by the Good News of Jesus.

MUSIC:
Give me oil in my lamp, keep me burning   JP50/MP167
One more step along the world I go   JP188
Though the world has forsaken God   JP257
This little light of mine   JP258

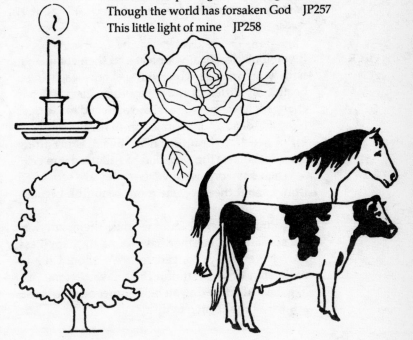

97

THEME: *Grief*

AIM: To prepare the children, as far as one is able, for the idea that they will one day (perhaps one or two have already experienced this) feel very sad and upset when someone they love dies.

AIDS: *If it is Autumn time, collect enough large leaves (Maples are perfect for this) that have fallen from the trees and are in multi-hues of gold and brown. Give each child a leaf. A reader.*

LEADER: If you look closely at your leaf and then compare it with your friend's you will see how each is so beautifully different from the other. Each leaf has changed; it was once green and attached to the tree. Now it is dead and separated from the tree.

But see how beautiful it is. Every living thing must die; that is the way God has allowed it to be.

When someone we love dies they are separated from us; but they become more beautiful, because they are with God.

We are sad then because we miss them; but they are not sad, because they have found the happiness they have always longed for. We should try to understand how beautiful they have become . . . like the leaf. How do you help someone who is sad at such a time? Listen to this:

BIBLE TEXT: *Jesus went in, took the girl by the hand and she got up.*
Matthew 9:25

READER: A little girl came home from a neighbour's house where her little friend had died.

"Why did you go?" questioned her father.

"To comfort her mother," replied the child.

"What could you do to comfort her?" the father continued.

"I climbed into her lap and cried with her," answered the child.

LEADER: That is all we can do; share a friend's sadness. But that is an important thing to do.

PRAYER FOCUS: *That we not leave our friends alone when they grieve, but be there for them. That Christ may take our hand when such sadness comes to us.*

MUSIC: Soon and very soon we are going to see the King
JP221/MP605

I do not know what lies ahead   JP92/MP269

Now be strong and very courageous   JP172

The Handicapped

AIM: To help children appreciate the needs of the handicapped and the contribution they can make to society.

AIDS: *A pair of spectacles. A reader.*

LEADER: If I take my spectacles off (or, anyone wearing a pair of spectacles like these) I am handicapped; I can see things which are very close but everything else is very hazy. I am handicapped and many people who wear glasses or use hearing aids are handicapped. We usually use the word for people who are more severely handicapped.

I want to tell you the true story of a young woman. She received a medal from the Queen, the MBE, for her work for the handicapped. She spent hours and hours writing letters to cheer them up and encourage them; she ran a club for them and told them how to get the benefits due to them. That was kind of her wasn't it? But the amazing thing is she was handicapped herself . . . Listen now to her story.

READER: Hilary Pole always wanted to be a teacher, a PE teacher. After her training she taught in a Midlands Secondary school; but before long she was taken very ill. It proved to be a very rare disease, called myasthenia. At first Hilary felt tired and floppy,

BIBLE TEXT: *I tell you the truth, whatever you did for one of the least of these brothers of mine, you did for me.* Matthew 25:40

then she was taken into hospital. She lost the use of her legs, arms and hands; and after a while even her voice. For the next thirteen years she lived unable to move any part of her body, even her eyes were closed. She learnt to communicate through the only movement left to her; she could only move the big toe of her left foot. It was only a tiny movement, one-sixteenth of an inch, but enough to touch an electric switch on a machine called a Possum, wired up to her toe.

For over ten years Hilary thought of others and worked for the handicapped. She wrote hundreds of letter and articles for people handicapped like herself. Then one day during a minor operation she died.

PRAYER FOCUS: *Thank you to God for the good health we have; help to respect those who are physically and mentally handicapped.*

MUSIC: Two little eyes to look to God   JP262
Thank You for every new good morning   JP230
Oh! Oh! Oh! how good is the Lord   JP180/MP532
(*see also Sight*)

Happiness

AIM: To help the children appreciate that loving and serving God (religion) is not meant to be dull and over serious.

AIDS: *Get some of the children to prepare a large poster, with a smiling face and the words, "If you see someone without a smile give them one of yours."*

LEADER: Children, if you look round you will see people here who are young and not so young; tall and short, men and women, etc. Everyone is uniquely different from everyone else. Now here is the question. What is it that everyone here wants? What would everyone here like to have?

Yes, the answer is HAPPINESS. Everyone wants to be happy.

Here is an old story about looking for happiness.

Once upon a time there was a medieval king who asked advice from a wise old man in his court. The king was very fed-up and depressed; he just could not cheer himself up; he kept thinking about all of his troubles and worries. So he called for the wise man and asked him how he might be really happy. The old man replied, "There is only one cure for the King. Your Majesty must sleep one night in the shirt of a happy man."

Messengers were dispatched by the king to

A happy heart makes the face cheerful.
                                    Proverbs 15:13

search for a man who was truly happy. But everyone who was approached had some anxiety and worry to spoil their happiness. At long last they found a beggar, who sat smiling by the roadside; he said that he was a really happy man with no worries. They offered him a very large sum of money for his shirt. The beggar burst into uncontrollable laughter, and replied. "I am sorry, I cannot help the King. I haven't got a shirt to sell him."

Having things does not bring happiness; having lots of things can bring unhappiness. The beggar had nothing and was perfectly happy; the king had everything, except happiness.

PRAYER
FOCUS:
God wants us to be happy; our happiness comes from him and through the loving of others, as he asks.

MUSIC:
Happiness is to know the Saviour   JP70
If I were a butterfly   JP94
I've got that joy, joy, joy   JP121

Harvest

AIM: To help the children appreciate that it is God the Creator who provides all the necessities of life.

AIDS: *The usual display of harvest gifts. A good reader.*

LEADER: When you have been to a friend's party, what do you say when you leave? Yes, you say "thank you". Why do you do that?

That is why we are here today, to say "thank you" to God for his goodness and kindness to us. We believe that everything that we have to make our lives possible – food, drink, homes, etc. – comes from his goodness. Now that we have supermarkets with food in them from all over the world, it is hard for us to understand how important harvest time was for the people of the past. Here is a reading from life in England, about one hundred years ago.

READER: At last, in the cool dusk of an August evening, the last load of corn was brought in, with a nest of merry boys' faces among the sheaves on the top of the yellow and blue painted farm wagons drawn by the big cart-horses and the men walking alongside with pitchforks on their shoulders. As they passed along the roads they shouted, "Harvest home. Harvest home. Merry, merry, merry, harvest home." Women came to their cottage gates and waved, and the few passers-by looked up and

BIBLE TEXT: *Give thanks to the Lord, for he is good.*

Psalm 106

smiled their congratulations. The joy and pleasure of the labourers in their task well done . . . they loved the soil and rejoiced in their work and skill in bringing forth the fruits of the soil, and harvest home put the crown on their year's work. (*Lark Rise to Candleford. F. Thompson*)

LEADER: Let us simply thank God for the farmers, wherever they live and work in the world, who grow the crops so that we can have bread to eat, fruit on our tables and vegetables for our dinners.

PRAYER
FOCUS: *Thanksgiving to God our Creator who provides all we need for life; help for all those who grow the food and provide it in our shops.*

MUSIC: Come, you thankful people, come   JP32/MP106
God, whose farm is all creation   JP61
Our harvest day is over for yet another year   JP193
We plough the fields and scatter   JP267/MP732

THEME: *Helpfulness*

AIM: To help the children appreciate that Christians do not help people just to be "nice" but because Christ asks it, and to assist a needy person is to assist Christ himself.

AIDS: *A cup of cold water, a gift-wrapped present.*

LEADER: Here I have a gift, beautifully wrapped, and a cup of water. Which would you prefer? Remember you have no idea what is in the gift-wrapped box. You prefer the gift, because the cup of water is boring, but imagine if you were very thirsty, you had not had anything to drink for a long time.

Which would you then choose?

Which would you choose if there was a big prize for choosing the cup of cold water?

Jesus says if we help someone in need, like giving a cup of cold water to a very thirsty peron, he will give us a reward. That must mean a reward in heaven. "Give," Jesus tells us (*Luke 6:38*), "and it will be given to you. A good measure, pressed down, shaken together and running over, will be poured into your lap."

So let us be helpful and be generous with our help.

BIBLE TEXT: *If anyone gives even a cup of cold water to one of these little ones . . . he will certainly not lose his reward.*

Matthew 10:42

PRAYER FOCUS: *Gratitude for the help we each receive from parents, teachers, etc; help to be generous in our caring for others; to see Christ in anyone who is in need.*

MUSIC:
A boy gave to Jesus   JP1
If you see someone lying in the road   JP95
Make me a servant, humble and meek   JP162
Make me a channel of your peace   JP161/MP456
(*see also* Helping)

Helping

To emphasize that to help other people makes it possible for quite big things to happen; even our little efforts can make a difference.

A long scarf, or a thick cord or rope tied to a firm chair or bench; this should be placed where all can see it. Seven children are needed, graded in size. First a big strong-looking boy, then a big girl, then a medium size boy and girl, and then two small and one very small child.

I expect many of you know the story of the enormous turnip; we are now going to retell it with the add of some volunteers.

One day in the spring an old man went out to sow some turnip seeds in his garden. It rained and the sun shone and as the weeks passed the old man noticed that one of this turnip plants was growing bigger and faster than the rest. It grew and grew and grew until it was simply enormous. No one had ever seen such an enormous turnip before.

One day the old man fancied some turnip for his dinner and went out in his garden to pull it up. (*The big boy comes out at this point and pretends to pull hard on the scarf or cord.*) He pulled and pulled but the enormous turnip would not come up; so the old man called his wife. (*Out comes the big girl to join the boy and both pull, one behind the other.*) The old man pulled, the old woman pulled with all their strength, but the turnip did not come up.

So the old woman called to a boy to come and help (*the medium size boy comes out*); the old man pulled, the old woman pulled and the boy pulled with all their strength, but the turnip did not come up. So the boy called to a girl to come and help (*the medium size girl comes out*), the old man pulled, the old woman pulled, the boy pulled and the girl pulled with all their strength, but the turnip did not come up. The girl called to a dog (*next child comes out*) to come and help; the old man pulled, the old woman pulled, the boy pulled, the girl pulled, the dog pulled with all their strength, but the turnip did not come up.

The dog called to a cat to come and help (*the next child comes out*); the old man pulled, the old woman pulled, the boy pulled, the girl pulled, the dog pulled and the cat pulled with all their strength, but the turnip did not come up. The cat called to a mouse (*the smallest child now joins the line*) to come and help; the old man pulled, the old woman pulled, the boy pulled, the girl pulled, the dog pulled, the cat pulled and the mouse pulled . . . and the turnip came out so suddenly that they all tumbled down on top of one another (*the line of children match the action to the words*) and burst out laughing. They all went into the house and shared a turnip meal together.

109

First, thank you to our actors who can return to their places. Now, what lesson do we learn from that story? Yes, it is only when the mouse helps that the turnip comes up. The smallest one in the line matters; the help of the mouse brought success for them all.

You may feel that your help at home or at school, is too little to matter; that is not so, as the story shows.

PRAYER
FOCUS:

We thank God that no matter how big or small we are we are loved equally by God. May we never hesitate to offer help to those in need.

MUSIC:

When I needed a neighbour   JP275
One more step along the world I go   JP188
Lord we ask how to receive your blessing   JP301
(*see also Helpfulness*)

Helping the Needy

AIM: To help the children appreciate that Christ sees all men and women as children of God, and a kindness to any one of them is a kindness to the Son of God.

AIDS: *None.*

LEADER: A traditional Portuguese story tells of a young man who travelled to the West Indies to seek his fortune. Nothing more was heard of him for a long time; eventually he returned to his home city of Lisbon with two of his own ships, both loaded with riches.

"Now," he thought, "I will play a trick on my relations." (His parents had died when he was child.) He put on some very worn old clothes and went to see his cousin Pedro.

"Here I am, your cousin John; after some years travelling the world I have come back home. Can I stay in your house just for a while until I get settled?" His cousin replied, "Ah, my dear John, how I wish I could help you, but there is not a free room in the house. Why don't you try Franco?"

So John went round to see his cousin Franco. There he received the same welcome. He tried two more cousins and an uncle and all declared how much they would like to help but they did not have a spare room or bed.

John returned to his two ships in the harbour. He put on his most expensive and fashionable

I tell you the truth, whatever you did for one of the least of these brothers of mine, you did for me.

Matthew 25:40

clothes and, accompanied by his secretary and two servants, went back into Lisbon. There he bought a large mansion in the main street. In a day or two his fabulous wealth was the talk of the city.

"Who would have imagined," his cousins, who had turned him away from their doors, said, "if only we had known about his treasure ships in the harbour; how differently we would have treated him. But it's no good now, we have spoilt our chance with him for ever."

We must remember that Christ Jesus comes to us in the same way, in the disguise of everyone and anyone in need. If we turn him away we will not share in his treasures of love and joy.

PRAYER
FOCUS:
That our eyes may be opened to how Christ comes to us; that we may have the generosity never to turn away anyone in need.

MUSIC:
When I needed a neighbour, were you there   JP275
If you see someone lying in the road   JP95
Make me a channel of your peace   JP161/MP456
(*see also Helping*)

Holidays

AIM: To help the children appreciate that God wants us to have holidays so that we can be re-created.

AIDS: *Some luggage; large and small suitcases and bags.*
       Three cards with the words, HOLY DAY HOLIDAY.

LEADER: (*Enter with the luggage, or turn away to pick up/load up with the luggage.*)
         Where do you think I'm going? Yes, but before I go off on holiday what preparations do you think I ought to make? (*Children suggest turning off the water, stopping the delivery of the newspaper etc.*)

         Did you know that before our time the only holidays people would get would be Sundays and special holy days. (*Hold up the two cards, apart*). These became known as a holyday. (*Hold two cards together, then substitute with the card with "holiday".*)

         So you see God and the Church have always been interested in the need we have for a rest from work. God himself rested on the seventh day, after creating the world.

         We need a time of rest to RE-CREATE ourselves; that is where the word "recreation" (*on a card?*) comes from.

BIBLE TEXT: *By the seventh day God had finished the work he had been doing; so on the seventh day he rested from all his work.*

Genesis 2:2

PRAYER
FOCUS:

Thanksgiving for holiday time; help for those who will not be able to have a holiday, because they are too poor or have to nurse a sick person, etc.

MUSIC:

In our work and in our play   JP108
Hushed was the evening hymn   JP85/MP253
For the beauty of the earth   JP48/MP152
(*see also Sunday*)

115

Holy Spirit

AIM: To help the children understand "the Holy Spirit" and the work of the Spirit.

AIDS: *A glove. A reader.*

LEADER: There is a story about a shoal of young fish who were told that if they swam in the ocean they would be happy. They went up to an old experienced shark and said, "Will you tell us where to go to find the ocean?" The shark replied, "You are in the ocean; be happy where you are." The young fish scoffed and laughed and swam off to find the ocean. The shark shrugged and got on with life.

Applied to the Holy Spirit the point of that story is that you do not have to go looking for the Holy Spirit, you already have that Spirit in your life. You see this glove on my hand; it only comes "alive" and does its job when I put it on (*match action to the words*).

Now you can seen the fingers of the glove moving. The glove can do nothing on its own; it needs the hand inside. So it is with the Holy Spirit. We are gloves and the Holy Spirit in us is the "hand" doing the good things.

What good things are you thinking? Here are some questions for you:

Can you tell the difference between a patient grown-up and an impatient one? You can?

BIBLE TEXT: *Since we live by the Spirit, let us keep in step with the Spirit.*

Galatians 5:25

Can you tell the difference between a loving and kind adult and an uncaring and unkind one? You can?

Can you tell the difference between someone who is gentle and self-controlled and someone who isn't? You can? Listen to this.

READER: The fruit of the Spirit is love, joy, peace, kindness, goodness, faithfulness, gentleness and self-control. (*Galatians 5:22*)

LEADER: The adults and children who show love, joy, peace, kindness have the Holy Spirit, like the hand in the glove, working in them. We have to give more and more room in our lives to the action of the Holy Spirit.

PRAYER FOCUS: *Thanksgiving for the Holy Spirit's presence in our lives; may we open ourselves more and more to growth in the Spirit.*

MUSIC: All over the world the Spirit is moving   JP5/MP18
Love, joy, peace and patience, kindness   JP158
Spirit of the Living God, fall afresh on me
    JP222/MP613
(*see also Pentecost*)

Humility

AIM: To introduce the children to the virtue of humility.

AIDS: *A reader*.

LEADER: Have you ever realized that Jesus was born in someone else's stable and, at the end of his life, he was buried in someone else's tomb? From the beginning of his life to the end Jesus was a very humble person. How do you think a humble person should behave? Here is a story about being humble and happy.

READER: If ever I'm disappointed with my lot in life, I stop and think about little Jamie Scott. Jamie was trying for a part in his school play. His mother told me that he'd set his heart on being in it, though she feared that he would not be chosen.

On the day the parts were awarded, I went with her to collect him after school. Jamie rushed out, eyes shining with pride and excitement. Then he said those words that remain a lesson to me, "I've been chosen to clap and cheer." (*Marie Curling*)

LEADER: It is interesting, isn't it, that the children who went home and boasted about having the principal parts have long been forgotten; but Jamie's happy and humble acceptance of his part has been written about and remembered.

BIBLE TEXT: *Everyone who exalts himself will be humbled and he who humbles himself will be exalted.*
Luke 14:11

PRAYER
FOCUS
Gratitude for all God's gifts; help to accept ourselves as we are and help to see ourselves as God sees us.

MUSIC:
Be still and know that I am God   JP22/MP48
Children of Jerusalem   JP24/MP70
Father, I place into your hands   JP42/MP133
(*see also Gentleness*)

AIM: To introduce the word and concept of the "Incarnation"; and how God came in Jesus but was not recognized by many.

AIDS: *A sheet of paper with the word INCARNATION. A reader.*

LEADER: As you grow older as Christians you will hear the word "Incarnation" used; here it is, so that you can see how it is spelt. It comes from two Latin words which mean, "in human flesh", in other words "one of us".

Here is an old Russian legend which will help you to understand the word.

READER: The Russians have a legend about a young medieval prince called Alexis, who lived in a sumptuous palace, while all around, in filthy hovels, lived hundreds of poor peasants. The Prince was a good young man and was moved by compassion for these poor folk; he was determined to improve their lives for them. So he began to visit them. Unfortunately as he moved among them he found that he had no point of contact with them; they treated him with enormous respect, almost worship; but he just could not gain their confidence and still less their affection and trust. He returned to the palace a defeated and disappointed young man.

Time passed and then one day a little older man came from a journey among the people. He was a

The world did not recognize him. He came to his own, but his own did not recognize him. John 1:11

rough and ready young doctor who also wanted to devote his life to the service of the poor. He rented a filthy rat-ridden shack on one of the back streets. He was one of them with no pretence to be different; he lived on the same simple food without knowing where the next meal was coming from. He made no money from his profession because he treated people free. Before long the young doctor had won the love and respect of all the people as Prince Alexis had never succeeded in doing. He was truly one of them. Little by little he transformed the whole spirit of the place; others imitated him and helped others freely. He settled quarrels and showed them love in action.

No one ever guessed the truth. The young doctor was in fact Prince Alexis who had abandoned his palace life to be one of them.

LEADER: That is what we celebrate in Jesus; God among us. He came down side by side with us to help us to become the sort of people he wants us to be.

PRAYER
FOCUS: *Thanksgiving for Jesus, the Son of God among us; that we may imitate the love of Jesus for all.*

MUSIC: Jesus is a friend of mine JP136
I danced in the morning JP91
Jesus is Lord! Creation's voice proclaims it JP137/MP367
(*see also Christ – Human Like Us*)

121

THEME: *Joy*

AIM: To help the children appreciate that you do not
           have to be solemn all the time to be good; joy and
           happiness can uplift and further God's work.

AIDS: *Five or six children with prepared jokes (written down to
           be read out, do not trust memories).*
           These come out at the beginning.

LEADER: Our theme today is JOY so we are beginning with
           some jokes the children would like to share . . .

CHILD A: Which dog has no tail? (*Reply*) A hot dog.

CHILD B: Why do birds fly south in the winter? (*Reply*)
           Because it is too far too walk.

CHILD C: How do farmers count their cows? (*Reply*) With
           cowculators. (*Etc*)

LEADER: There is the story of the Irishman who died
           suddenly and went up for divine judgement,
           feeling extremely uneasy. He didn't think that he
           had done much good on earth. There was a queue
           ahead of him, so he settled down to look and listen.
           After consulting his big book, Christ said to the first
           man in the line, "I see here that I was hungry and
           you gave me something to eat. Good man, come
           into heaven." To the second he said, "I read here
           that I was thirsty and you gave me a drink; well
           done, come into heaven."

122

The Irishman was very worried, he felt that he had much to fear because he had never given anyone food or a drink; or visited them in prison or when they were sick. Then his turn came. Trembling he watched as Christ examined the book of judgement. Then Christ looked up and said, "Well, there's not much written here, but you did do something. I was sad and discouraged and depressed and you cheered me up with your jokes. Get along into heaven."

There is a lovely point to the story; to cheer up another person who is depressed is to cheer up Christ.

PRAYER
FOCUS:

Thanksgiving for all those things – music, fun and laughter – that brighten our lives; may we put ourselves out to make others happy.

MUSIC:

If you want joy, real joy   JP96
I've got that joy, joy, joy, joy   JP121
Give me oil in my lamp (verses 2/3)   JP50/MP167
The joy of the Lord is my strength   JP240
(*see also Happiness*)

Judging by Appearances

AIM:

To correct the common assumption, that the children will acquire, that you can judge someone by appearances.

AIDS:

A large paper sack used for potatoes, and a pair of scissors.

LEADER:

Everyone enjoys a good story, and fantasy stories are particularly popular. Here is a modern fairy story. It is called the "Paperbag Princess".

Once upon a time there was a beautiful young princess, named Georgina. She lived with her parents in a large castle. The young man that she loved and was going to marry was visiting her home, with his parents, when the tragedy occurred. His name was Prince Harold; and he was very particular about how he dressed; he was always combing his hair.

Then disaster struck. A huge dragon attacked the castle and blasted everything in sight; everything was destroyed. When Georgina pulled herself out of the rubble she discovered two things: the dragon had gone with Harold and she had no clothes to wear. Georgina was very angry, she had to rescue Harold. She looked for something to wear and could only find a brown paper bag.

(Produce the paper bag and cut out the two bottom corners to match the story)

BIBLE TEXT: *Man looks at the outward appearance,*
but the Lord looks at the heart.

1 Samuel 16:7

Georgina found an old pair of scissors and cut the corners to make a dress; her face was still dirty and her hair a mess, but she set off immediately to seek Harold.

It was not hard to track the dragon – he left a trail of destruction. After many miles Georgina found the dragon's cave. Without a thought for her own safety Georgina hammered on the massive door. After a while it opened just enough for the dragon to peep out. "Go away, little girl," the dragon said, "I'm very tired." He slammed the door shut. Georgina carried on knocking. "Go away," said the dragon when he opened the door again. This time Georgina spoke, "Are you the famous dragon that can fly around the world in ten seconds?" The dragon was interested. "Yes," he replied, "I am that dragon." "I don't believe you," said Georgina. "I can," answered the dragon indignantly. "Prove it," taunted the girl. Out came the dragon to prove his ability. "Remember," said Georgina, "in ten seconds." Woosh . . . the dragon was off. One, two, three . . . Georgina counted the time.

Woosh . . . the dragon was back. "Brilliant," said the princess, "exactly ten seconds. I bet you couldn't do it again." "I'm very tired," replied the dragon. "Never mind," taunted Georgina, "I knew you couldn't do it." Without another word the dragon was off again. This time he took fourteen

125

seconds. When he arrived back he was shattered, he collapsed on the ground and went fast asleep.

Georgina tip-toed up to the dragon and checked that he really was asleep. Then she pushed open the door of the cave and went in. There at the back of the cave, safe and sound, was Harold. "Hello," he called, "you've been a long time." Georgina found some keys and let Harold out. As they stepped out of the cave and over the body of the dragon, Harold said, "Goodness me, Georgina, just look at you. Your hair is in a mess and your face is terrible, and what are you wearing? I couldn't marry anyone who dresses like that."

Georgina was angry, very angry indeed. "I wouldn't marry you," she replied, "if you were the last man in world." And she stormed off home on her own.

Well, children, what do you think? Was she right? Yes, of course. She had shown such love and concern; she had been very brave risking her own life and she had cleverly tricked the dragon. Harold did not even say thank you; all he was interested in was how she was dressed.

PRAYER
FOCUS:

That we may not judge anyone by what they wear. That we may, as God does, look for the love in every one's actions.

MUSIC: There are hundreds of sparrows   JP246
              The greatest thing in all my life is knowing you
                 JP239/MP646
              Have you see the pussy cat   JP72
              If I were a butterfly   JP94

The Kingdom of God

AIM:
To help the children understand the phrase which is constantly being heard in worship "the Kingdom of God".

AIDS:
The story below can be acted out successfully, or mimed while a narrator reads the text. If the "Leader" is going to read or tell the story he/she could give (availability permitting) a single marigold to each child; or ask them to take a marigold and present it to the elderly in church.

LEADER/
READER:
Some children were at play in their playground one day, when a herald rode through the town, blowing a trumpet, and crying aloud, "The King! The King passes by this road today. Make ready for the King!" The children stopped their play, and looked at one another. "Did you hear that?" they said. "The King is coming. He may look over the wall and see our playground; who knows? We must put it in order."

The playground was sadly dirty, and in the corners were scraps of paper and broken toys, for these were careless children. But now, one brought a hoe, and another a rake, and a third ran to fetch the wheelbarrow from behind the garden gate. They laboured hard, till at length all was clean and tidy. "Now it is clean!" they said; "but we must make it pretty, too, for kings are used to fine things;

maybe he would not notice mere cleanness, for he may have it all the time."

Then one brought sweet rushes and strewed them on the ground; and others made garlands of oak leaves and fine tassels and hung them on the walls; and the littlest one pulled marigold buds and threw them all about the playground, "to look like gold," he said. When all was done the playground was so beautiful that the children stood and looked at it, and clapped their hands with pleasure. "Let us keep it always like this!" said the littlest one; and the others cried. "Yes! Yes! That is what we will do."

They waited all day for the coming of the King, but he never came; only, towards sunset, a man with travel-worn clothes, and a kind face passed along the road and stopped to look over the wall. "What a pleasant place!" said the man. "May I come in and rest, dear children?" The children brought him in gladly, and set him on the seat that they had made out of an old cask. They had covered it with the old red cloak to make it look like a throne, and it made a very good one.

'It is our playground!" they said. "We made it pretty for the King, but he did not come, and now we mean to keep it so for ourselves." "That is good!" said the man. "Because we think pretty and clean is nicer than ugly and dirty!" said another.

"That is better!" said the man. "And for tired people to rest in!" said the littlest one. "That is best of all!" said the man.

He sat and rested, and looked at the children with such kind eyes that they came about him, and told him all they knew; about the five puppies in the barn, and the thrush's nest with four blue eggs, and the field where the marigolds grew; and the man nodded and understood all about it.

By and by he asked for a cup of water, and they brought it to him in the best cup, with the gold sprigs on it; then he thanked the children, and rose and went on his way; but before he went he laid his hand on their heads for a moment, and the touch went warm to their hearts.

The children stood by the wall and watched the man as he went slowly along. The sun was setting, and the light fell in long slanting rays across the road. "He looks so tired!" said one of the children. "But he was so kind!" said another. "See!" said the littlest one. "How the sun shines on his hair! It looks like a crown of gold." (*Laura E. Richards*)

LEADER: That lovely story, as I am sure you realize, is about the way Christ our King comes into our lives quietly, humbly, through others. Inspiring us to help others and improve conditions around us.

That is what "the Kingdom of God" or "the Kingdom of Heaven" means when you hear it in our readings from the Bible.

The "Kingdom" is not a place it is a "Kingship" or a reigning of Christ among us by love.

PRAYER
FOCUS:

That we all open our hearts to true unselfish love and look for opportunities to help our parents, our brothers and sisters, friends and anyone we meet in the course of the day.

MUSIC:

How lovely on the mountains   JP84/MP249
I want to walk with Jesus Christ   JP124/MP302
Majesty, worship His Majesty   JP160/MP454

THEME: *Knowing Yourself*

AIM: To encourage the children to think about them-selves and their relationship with God.

AIDS: *A large mirror and a large card with some words printed in large letters, ("God knows me" or "God loves me").*
A ballet shoe, a football boot, a broom and a hammer (or similar objects).

LEADER: *(Mirror is positioned where all can see what it reflects.)* Can you read what I have printed on this card? Yes, "God loves me". Now, if I hold it up to the mirror can you read what it says. No, it's back to front. The words are round the wrong way.

Do you realise what that means? It means that you have never seen yourself as you really are. What you see in the mirror is round the wrong way; your face is not the same as you really are; as other people see you.

There is no need to worry; God knows me and you intimately. He knows what we are like, deep down inside ourselves.

(Hold up the ballet shoes.) What are these used for? Yes, but could I do ballet in these *(hold up the football boots)*? No, of course not. Ballet shoes are for ballet and football boots for playing football.

If I want to sweep the kitchen floor do I use this? *(Hold up the hammer.)* No, that is for hammering in nails. I use this broom. Everything is made for a purpose.

What has God made me for? Yes, you and I have been made by God for a purpose. We can only be happy people if we know and try to live according to that purpose.

God has made me to know him, love him and serve him.

More important than how I look is to know why I am here, why God, using my parents, created me in the first place. When we really appreciate that, we can live a really happy life.

PRAYER   *Thank God for being here, just the way I am; help to*
FOCUS: *understand why I am here; to grow in knowledge and love*
              of God.

MUSIC: He gave me eyes so I could see   JP74
              If I were a butterfly   JP94
              Father, I place into your hands   JP42/MP133

Leadership

AIM: To help the children appreciate that Christ's words can apply to them; if they follow the lead and example of some of their friends they could get into trouble.

AIDS: *None.*

LEADER: I am sure you have heard the story of Chicken Licken. Well, just to remind you of this old and traditional story, it goes like this:

Once there was a little chicken who was known as Chicken Licken. One day an acorn fell on his head and Chicken Licken thought the sky was falling down; so he ran off to tell the King.

On the way he met a hen, called Henny Penny. Chicken Licken said, "The sky is falling down"; and Henny Penny said, "I'd better go with you to tell the king."

Further on they met, the cockerel, Cocky Locky. Chicken Licken said, "The sky is falling down"; and Cocky Locky said, "I'd better go with you to tell the King."

As Henny Penny and Cocky Locky followed Chicken Licken they met a duck, Ducky Lucky.

Chicken Licken said, "The sky is falling down"; and Ducky Lucky said, "I'd better go with you to tell the King." They all followed Chicken Licken and met the goose, Goosey Loosey. Chicken Licken said, "The sky is falling down"; and Goosey Loosey

Can a blind man lead a blind man?
Will they not both fall into a pit?

Luke 6:39

said, "I'd better go with you to tell the King."

Well, on they went and they met Turkey Lurkey as well, who also joined the line following Chicken Licken.

A little further on they met a fox, called Foxy Loxy. "Where are you all going in such a hurry?" he asked. "Oh, Foxy Loxy," said Chicken Licken, "we are on our way to tell the King that the sky is falling down."

"I know where to find the King," said Foxy Loxy, "You had better all follow me." And the fox led them all straight into his den where they were gobbled up by the fox family.

How silly they all were. They followed a leader without question; no one stopped to ask Chicken Licken more about why he thought the sky was falling down or who this "king" was and where he could be found. A blind leader led blind followers. You can so easily do the same; never follow the leadership of a friend without question; think for yourself, remember your own Christian standards and ideals.

PRAYER
FOCUS:

Thanks for friends who help and encourage us; help to choose friends wisely and not follow anyone blindly.

MUSIC:

Make me a channel of your peace   JP161/MP456
This little light of mine   JP258
Give me oil in my lamp   JP50/MP167

THEME: *Listen*

AIM: To help the children understand that prayer does not just involve asking, but also listening.

AIDS: *A radio.*

LEADER: Do you all know what this is? What will happen if I switch it on? Is the music only here when I put the radio on or all the time? Yes, the radio waves are passing through the air all the time. We cannot see the radio waves but they are there and they are picked up by the radio so that we can hear them. What we listen to is there all the time, whether we tune in or not.

It is just the same with God. He is there all the time; all we have to do is to "tune" in to him. If we turn our minds and our hearts to God, in other words if we think of God and want to listen to him and talk to him, then we are in immediate contact with God.

To listen to the radio we only have to turn on and tune in. To listen to God and pray, all we have to do is turn our attention to God and tune our thoughts in to his.

PRAYER FOCUS: *Gratitude to God for always being there, always available to us; help to remember this and act on it.*

136

BIBLE TEXT: *My sheep listen to my voice; I know them, and then follow me.* John 10:27

MUSIC: Be still and know that I am God   JP22/MP48
Isaiah heard the voice of the Lord   JP114
Jesus is knocking, patiently waiting   JP135
Hushed was the evening hymn   JP85/MP253

Little Sins

AIM: To help children appreciate that even little wrong-doings can hurt us and our friendship with God.

AIDS: *A large stone or housebrick, and a collection of at least ten small stones or pebbles. The large stone or brick is placed on the floor in view and the small stones are distributed around the area. A reader.*

LEADER: Which stone can be seen by everyone?

I would like one of you to pick up the big stone and one of you to go around and pick up the small stones.

Now that has been done, let me explain and then we will listen to a story. The stones represent, stand for, the sins that people can commit. A big sin, like stealing a lot of money, can be seen by many people. Little sins, like the small stones are not noticed. But, does that mean that they are not important?

If we claim to be without sin, we deceive ourselves and the truth is not in us. 1 John 1:8

READER: This is an old traditional story.

Two men went to visit a holy man for advice. "Can you tell us what we must do to be forgiven our sins?"

"You must tell God that you are sorry," said the holy man, "and he will forgive you."

"We have done that," replied one of the visitors, "and we still feel bad."

'Tell me of your wrong-doing, my sons," said the old man.

The first man said, "I have committed a great and grievous sin."

The second man said, "I have done a lot of wrong things, but they were all small and not important."

"This is what you must do," said the holy man. "You must go and get me a stone that represents each of your sins."

The first man came back with a big stone and the second man came back with a bag of small stones.

"Now," said the old man, "take all those stones and put them back where you found them."

The first man picked up his big rock and staggered back to where he had found it. But the second man could only remember where a few of his pebbles had lain; he came back and said the task was too difficult.

"You must know," said the holy old man, "that sins are like these stones. If a person has committed a big sin, it lies like a heavy stone on his conscience; if he is truly sorry, he is forgiven and the load is taken away. But if a person is always doing small things that are wrong, he does not feel very guilty, so he is not sorry. So you see, it is important to avoid little sins as well a big ones." (*Anonymous*)

LEADER: Would those with the stones now try to put them back exactly where they found them?

PRAYER
FOCUS: *Thankfulness to God for his generous willingness to forgive us when we are truly sorry; help to be sorry for all the little things we do that are wrong.*

MUSIC: Amazing grace! How sweet the sound   JP8/MP31
           O sinner man, where will you run to?   JP194
           God forgave my sin in Jesus' name   JP54/MP181

THEME: *Little Things*

AIM: To help the children understand that little things in
           life – the small everyday actions that seem to be
           boring – can be important and valuable, to help us
           in our growth in the Christian life.

AIDS: *A packet of very small seeds (particularly valuable if
           the seed grows into a large plant, e.g. broccoli). A
           reader?*

LEADER: I have been round to each of you and poured a few
           seeds from this packet into the palm of your hand.
           According to the picture on the front, each one of
           those tiny seeds will grow unto a tall plant. Does
           anyone know how big a broccoli plant will grow?
           Yes, as tall as you.

           Here is a true story about using seeds to change a
           whole stretch of countryside.

LEADER   Elezard Bouffier was a simple and uneducated
(OR   shepherd. He lived in France in an area called
READER):   Provence. Elezard was a shepherd in a very barren
           area with very very few plants and trees; it was only
           suitable country for a herd of sheep. Elezard had no
           family and lived all alone.

           It was the year 1910 and Elezard had an idea. In
           the autumn, as he cared for his flock under the few
           oak trees, he picked up every acorn that he found
           and took them back to his hut, where he kept them
           dry.

BIBLE TEXT: *If you have faith as small as a mustard seed.*
Matthew 17:20

In the early spring, as he walked with his flock he would prod a hole in the ground with his shepherd's crook and drop in one of the acorns he was carrying. He did this every autumn and spring for thirty-seven years; and gradually the whole barren area was transformed. The trees grew, an undergrowth developed and the countryside teemed with birds and wildlife. At Elezard's death in 1947 a whole region of Provence had been totally changed and today it is the pleasant site of a new housing development with protected parks and countryside walks.

PRAYER FOCUS: *That we may all realize how important all the little things of life are. How grateful we must be for the gift of our faith; may it grow day by day as a seed grows into a tall plant.*

MUSIC: Two little eye to look to God   JP262
This little light of mine   JP258
Thank you for ev'ry new good morning   JP230

THEME: *Living Water*

AIM: To help the children appreciate the use of the symbol or sign of water in the Scriptures.

AIDS: *Pictures (either cut from magazines or drawn) of various uses of water; e.g. a washing machine, a shower, a bath, someone cleaning their teeth, etc.*

LEADER: Is there anyone here who does not like washing? Why is it important to wash? What would happen if you did not wash? What do we use for washing?

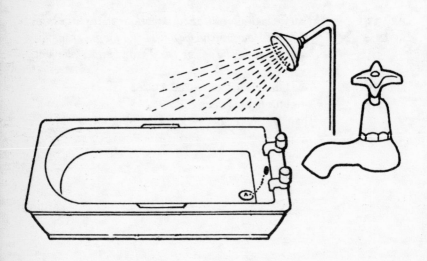

BIBLE TEXT: *Whoever believes in me, as the Scripture has said, streams of living water will flow from within him.*

John 7:38

Can anyone remember a time when they were very thirsty? Why do we have to drink? Yes, washing and drinking are important for everyday life. (*Show the pictures.*) Here are some pictures showing how important water is for our everyday life.

Did you know that in the country of the Bible it only rains twice a year, and sometimes only once? The Jewish people prayed, and still do, for it to rain so that they could grow their crops. If water did not come from the skies then their crops would not grow, and death would follow. So water is the perfect symbol of life.

In baptism we go down into the water and rise up out of the water to a new life.

(*Give out the pictures.*) Now, on the back of the picture write these words (*on a poster so that little ones can copy*)

"Thank you God for water, and life."

PRAYER
FOCUS:

Thanksgiving for water and all that it does for us in our lives; help to share our faith with others so that they live by faith in Jesus.

MUSIC:

Have you heard the raindrops drumming on the
    rooftops? JP71
Wide, wide as the ocean JP292
Deep and wide, deep and wide JP35

Loneliness

AIM: To help the children appreciate that while everyone is lonely sometimes, Christians have a close personal friend in Jesus.

AIDS: *A good reader.*

LEADER: Are you ever lonely? When do you feel most lonely?

    Do older people get lonely too?

    Do you think Jesus was ever lonely?

    Do you think it is very lonely if you are blind and unable to go out of your house?

    Here is the story of a person who should have been very lonely but did her best to overcome it.

    Hilary Pole was an ordinary little girl who grew up wanting to be a PE teacher. She achieved her ambition and started teaching at secondary school; then something very very unusual happened. She caught a very rare disease, an illness that took away her eyesight, her ability to walk, to hold a pen, to feel any sensation in her body or even to speak. She lay in bed and could hear, but she could not "talk" to anyone. She was only able to move the big toe of her right foot; and she could only move that a tiny amount, just a little flicker of movement.

    Many people would have given up; Hilary didn't.

146

Praise be to the Lord, who has not left you without a kinsman-redeemer.
Ruth 4:14

They gave her a Possum machine which allowed her to type messages to people. She wrote lots of letters to handicapped people to cheer them up. Instead of being totally cut off in a loneliness which we can hardly imagine, she made lots of friends and wrote poetry. Here is one of Hilary's poems:

READER:

I'm often asked if I am bored,
Frustrated, lonely,
My life abhorred,
And so I answer,
"I am not" –
That now I can accept my lot,
Remind the sadly shaking head,
"It is my body, not my mind, in bed."

I'm rarely frightened or in pain,
For this
I thank my God again.
I have many loyal friends,
My joy in them despair transcends.
There's music too,
Books to read.
Discontentment cannot breed.

LEADER: How can we complain about being lonely when we can see, run about and enjoy ourselves? Hilary had a great love of God and knew that Jesus, her friend, was with her at all times. We should remember that, too.

PRAYER FOCUS: *Thankfulness for good health, family and friends, and the special friendship of Jesus; help to develop our friendships, especially with Jesus, so that we have an answer to loneliness.*

MUSIC: What a friend we have in Jesus   JP273/MP746
            Whether you're one or whether you're two   JP284
            Jesus is a friend of mine   JP136
            If you see someone lying in the road   JP95
            (see also Dignity, and Special Person)

The Lord's Prayer

AIM: To help the children appreciate that the Lord's Prayer is a community prayer; not a prayer for oneself alone.

AIDS: *Perhaps an older child to read the poem.*

LEADER: You all know that Jesus himself taught us the prayer which we call the Lord's prayer, or the "Our Father". This has been called the family prayer of all Christians because every child of God has the right and privilege to say that prayer, whatever Christian church or tradition he or she belongs to. Have you ever realized that the words "I" and "me" do not occur once in the Lord's Prayer?

Yet while saying the "Our Father" it is easy to mean "my Father"; to say the words, "give us this day our daily bread" and still think only that it means, "give me my daily bread".

Here is a poem by Charles Thompson which may help us to realize that we should not be full of ourselves when we pray.

BIBLE TEXT: *This, then, is how you should pray:*
'Our Father in heaven, hallowed be your name . . .''

Matthew 6:9

READER:
You can not pray the Lord's Prayer,
And even once say "I".
You can not pray the Lord's Prayer,
And even once say "My".
Nor can you pray the Lord's Prayer,
And not pray for another;
For when you ask for daily bread,
You must include your brother.
For others are included
In each and every plea:
From the beginning to the end of it,
It does not once say "Me".

PRAYER
FOCUS:
Thanksgiving for the Lord's prayer; then say it slowly
together.

MUSIC:
Our Father who is in heaven   JP192/MP552
Father we love you   JP45/MP142
Father I place into your hands   JP42/MP133
Dear Lord and Father of mankind   JP37/MP111
(*see also Prayer, and Teach us to Pray*)

THEME: *Lost and Found*

AIM: To show that however far we may drift away from God he, like a loving shepherd, will always come looking for us.

AIDS: *Enough sheep shaped cut-outs, one for each of the children. A pencil. A reader.*

READER: Is there a farmer with a hundred sheep who wouldn't leave them on the moors – if he had lost just one of them? Wouldn't he go after that lost sheep until he found it?

When he finds it, how happy he is. He puts it on his shoulders and brings it home. He calls his friends and neighbours together. "I've found the lost sheep," says he. "Let's celebrate." (*Alan Dale*)

LEADER: Hands up anyone who has, at some time in the past, got lost. In a big shop, or in a park or perhaps in a new school. It's frightening, isn't it? But how did you feel when you were found?

That's what Jesus says happens. When the farmer or the shepherd finds his sheep, he comes home and says, "Let's celebrate"; because he is so happy.

If we ever wander away from God, like a sheep, God will be looking for us to return.

Now on the back of the sheep cut-out you have, please write the name of a friend who you know does not go to church, any church. We are going to

BIBLE TEXT: *Rejoice with me, I have found my sheep that was lost.*

Luke 15:6

collect them up and put them close to me during the rest of our service. We will pray that your friend will be found by the Good Shepherd and will get to know and love God.

PRAYER
FOCUS: *Thanksgiving that we belong to the flock of Christ; ask for the strength to remain true and loyal to the Good Shepherd throughout our lives. Prayer for our friends who do not yet know the love of Christ.*

MUSIC: The Lord's my Shepherd, I'll not want   JP243/MP660
    also JP241/MP649 *and* JP244
Put your hand in the hand of the man who stilled the water   JP206
When the road is rough and steep   JP279
(see also Loneliness)

THEME: *Love*

AIM: To bring out, for the children, the importance of love in their lives.

AIMS: *Four large pieces of card or sheets of paper with the letters L, O, V, E. Give out the card to four selected children in this order – V O L E. The children are invited to come out and show their letters in that order.*

LEADER: Does anyone know what a VOLE is? Yes, it is like a mouse. They live in burrows where they build a nest and have as many as 8 or 9 little babies.

Do you think they look after their babies? Yes, they do. (*Letters are put down.*) Now listen to this true story.

BIBLE TEXT: *As you have heard from the beginning, his command is that you walk in love.* 2 John 6

READER:　A twelve-year-old boy named Leo (*letter L held up*) went to visit his auntie during the Easter holidays at Orpington (*letter O is shown beside the L*). His auntie had a long garden and next door there was a very overgrown garden with an old van (*the letter V is shown*) at the bottom of the garden. It belonged to a middle-aged woman who lived on her own in the house next door.

Leo went exploring and got through the fence into the next garden. He had heard some strange noises and went to inspect the old broken down van in the undergrowth.

He found the rusty old van had a slit cut out in the back door and a dark piece of material hung on the inside over the slit. Leo found a stick and pushed it into the slit. Something inside grabbed the stick and pulled it. Leo let go and in fright ran back into his aunt's garden; right into his aunt who was looking for him. He blurted out what had happened. Now his aunt had been suspicious of the noises from the disused van for a very long time, so she rang the police.

The owner of the house denied that there was anything in the van; but the two policemen insisted on looking. It took several minutes to get the door open; when they did the mess inside was terrible and the smell almost unbearable. A strange creature lurked in one corner away from the light. It

155

was on all fours; it was naked, with long black hair and staring eyes. It was taken away and proved to be the eight-year-old son of the woman, who admitted that the child had been locked in the van for the last six years. It could not speak and was frightened of all other humans. The mother, who was eventually sent to prison for what she had done, had given her child no name, so it was called Elliot, after one of the policemen who discovered him (*letter E is shown*).

LEADER: That dreadful story is true. The woman had not even given her son a name; but worst of all she had given him no love. Without love we would all be like Elliot, neglected and less than human. In our prayers today let us thank God for all the love we have experienced and will experience in our lives.

PRAYER
FOCUS:
Gratitude for all the love which has been given to us and help us to grow as full human beings; help to return that love to our parents and our families.

MUSIC:
Jesus' love is very wonderful JP139
He brought me to his banqueting house JP73
Wide, wide as the ocean JP292
(*see also Loving God, and Loving our Neighbour*)

THEME:

Loving God

This is especially useful for Valentine's Day,
Mother's Day and Good Friday.

AIM:

To help the children understand the different kinds of love that there are; and the importance of our love of God.

AIDS:

Three large pieces of cardboard cut out in the shape of a heart (coloured red on one side) with words, on the reverse of each card:
Mother's Day on one, St Valentine's Day on the next, and Good Friday on the third.
Three children stand in full view, some distance apart, showing the hearts they are holding.

LEADER:

Today we are thinking about love, and you can see three hearts; that is because we alway link human love with the heart. When can you buy greetings cards in the shops with a heart on? Yes, on St Valentine's Day. (*Child with those words on his/her card turns the cards round to view.*) Did anyone get a card this year from a friend?

Not long after St Valentine's Day there is another day when we send cards that have the words "I love you" on them. When is that? That's right, on Mother's Day. (*Child with Mothers' Day heart turns it round.*)

BIBLE TEXT: *God is love. Whoever lives in love lives in God, and God in him.* 1 John 4:16

Why don't we send a Valentine's Day card to our mothers on Mother's Day? Both cards say "I love you". It's a different kind of love, isn't it.

Not many weeks after Mother's Day we Christians have a special day when we think about the great love Jesus had for us. What is it called? Yes, Good Friday. We do not send cards but it is a special day when we think of the love that Jesus showed us, by dying on the cross. (*Child with the third heart turns the words to view.*)

Three hearts . . . three different and important kinds of love: Romantic love – Family love – Love of God. We cannot live a healthy and happy life without love for our parents and family; love of friends and love of God.

PRAYER FOCUS: *Thanksgiving for God's great love of us, and the love of family and friends; that we may grow maturely in each of these loves.*

MUSIC:
I'm very glad of God   JP107
The greatest thing in all my life   JP239/MP646
He brought me to his banqueting house   JP73
(*see also Love, and Loving Our Neighbour*)

THEME: *Loving Our Neighbour*

AIM: To help the children appreciate how important it is not just to "love" those people we like, but everyone.

AIDS: *Heart-shaped pieces of paper, one for each child.*
A Reader.

LEADER: Tell me about the people that you love most. (*Accept ideas from the children*).

Is it possible to love a complete stranger? No it isn't, is it? And it could be dangerous to be friendly with a stranger, so take note of what you are told about speaking to strangers. But what about people in your class at school who you do not like, can you love them? Not easy, is it? But Jesus said we should care for them and show some concern, especially if they need help. Listen to this very famous story of Jesus'.

READER: Story of the Good Samaritan (*a child's version if possible*). Luke 10:25

LEADER: The Jews and the Samaritans, at the time of that story, were enemies; they hated one another. Who do people in our community, our society, look down on and despise these days? (*Accept suggestions.*) Now on the heart-shape that you have write one of the groups of people we have just talked about. (*Help with spelling, if necessary.*)

Now underneath write these words (*already prepared on a sheet*) "Help me to be kind to everyone".

PRAYER
FOCUS: *Gratitude for the love that we all experience in our families; help to be kind and caring about everyone, no matter how different they are from us.*

MUSIC: When I needed a neighbour   JP275
Make me a channel of your peace   JP161/MP456
(*see also Love, and Loving God*)

THEME: *Mercy*

AIM: To help the children understand the concept of mercy; their own need for it.

AIDS: *None.*

LEADER: How do you get on with your school teacher?

Do you have a strict Head Teacher?

This is the story of a boy who was sent to the Head Teacher of his school.

The boy was sent to the Head Teacher for breaking a school rule. After hearing the facts the Head Teacher took out a blank exercise book and wrote the boy's name, saying as he did so, "You have not been sent to me before. Now, I don't know you very well; you may really be a good boy, for all I know. Good boys sometimes make mistakes. Now I'll just make a note in pencil that you have been sent to me today, and I will also note why you were sent. But you see I am making this note in pencil so that it can easily be rubbed out. If you are not sent to be again this year, I shall erase this from my book and no one will ever know anything about it."

It was a lesson in mercy that the boy never forgot.

BIBLE TEXT: *The Lord is full of compassion and mercy.*
                                            James 5:11

PRAYER   *Thankfulness for God's continual kindness to us; help to*
FOCUS: *appreciate the need we have for God's loving mercy, and*
                the need we have to show the same kindness to others.

MUSIC: Let us with a gladsome mind   JP154/MP415
                Surely goodness and mercy shall follow me   JP223
                I'm very glad of God   JP107

Mother's Day (1)

AIM:

To help the children appreciate that they must care for and think about the needs of their mothers, as their mothers do for them.

AIDS:

A reader.

LEADER:

It is wonderful to think that one of the last things that Jesus did, just before he died, was to take care of his mother. The apostle John was asked to take care of her, like a son. We have a reading today which is a made-up, imaginative story of how God came to make a mother.

BIBLE TEXT: *Jesus said to his mother, standing near the cross, "Dear woman, here is your son," and to the disciple John, he said, "Here is your mother." From that time on, this disciple took Mary into his home.*   John 19:27

READER:

When the good Lord was creating mothers, he was into his sixth day of overtime when an angel appeared and said, "You're doing a lot of fiddling around on this one." And the Lord said, "Have you read the specifications on this order? She has to be completely washable, but not plastic . . . have 180 movable parts – all replaceable . . . run on black coffee and left-overs . . . have a lap that disappears when she stands up . . . a kiss that can cure anything from a broken leg to a disappointed love affair . . . and six pairs of hands."

The angel shook his head slowly and said, "Six pairs of hands? No way." "It's not the hands that are causing me problems," said the Lord, "It's the three pairs of eyes that mothers have to have." "That's on the standard model?" asked the angel. The Lord nodded, "One pair that sees through closed doors when she asks, 'What are you children doing in there?' When she already knows. Another in the back of her head that sees what she shouldn't, but what she has to know. And, of course, the ones in front that can look at a child when he or she gets into trouble and say, 'I understand and I love you,' without so much as uttering a word."

"Lord," said the angel, touching his sleeve gently, "go to bed. Tomorrow is another . . ." "I can't, " said the Lord, "I'm so close now. Already I

165

have one who heals herself when she is sick, can feed a family of six on one pound of mince, and can get a nine-year-old to have a bath."

The angel circled the model of a mother very slowly. "It's too soft," he sighed. "But tough," said the Lord excitedly. "You cannot imagine what this mother can do or endure." "Can it think?" asked the angel. "Not only think, but it can reason and compromise," said the Creator.

Finally the angel bent over and ran his finger across the cheek. "There's a leak," he pronounced. "It's not a leak," said the Lord. "It's a tear." "What's it for?" "It's for joy, sadness, disappointment, pain, loneliness and pride." "You are a genius," said the angel. The Lord looked sombre. "I didn't put it there." (*Anonymous*)

Need a 'prototype' volunteer.

Thanksgiving for mothers and grandmothers; help to be caring and thoughtful towards them in the future.

MUSIC: For the beauty of the earth   JP48/MP152
          Father I place into your hands   JP42/MP133
          I will sing, I will sing a song unto the Lord   JP126/MP313
          (see also Mother's Day (2), and Father's Day (1) and (2))

THEME:	*Mother's Day (2)*

AIM:	To help the children appreciate that they must care for and think about the needs of their mothers, as their mothers do for them.
AIDS:	*A vase full of flowers.*
LEADER:	Please put you hand up if your mother takes you or used to take you to school every day. (*Take one flower from the vase.*) That must be rewarded with a flower.

Hands up if your mother prepares your dinner every day. (*Take another flower.*) We ought to say thank you for that with a flower.

Hands up if your mother makes your bed every day. (*Another flower.*)

Hands up if your mother washes your clothes. (*Flower.*)

Hands up if your mother ever buys you sweets and toys. (*Flower.*)

Hands up if your mother helps you with school work. (*Flower.*)

Hands up if your mother, when you were tiny, fed you and washed you. (*Flower.*)

(*Continue with similar ideas until the Leader has a bunch of flowers.*)

See what a large "thank you" we should give to our mothers today. But not only today, every day.

Let us now present this bouquet of flowers to the oldest grandmother here today. (*A child does this.*).

BIBLE TEXT: *A woman in the crowd called out to Jesus, "Blessed is the mother who gave you birth."* Luke 11:27

PRAYER
FOCUS: *Thanksgiving for mothers and grandmothers and the love that they show us; help to appreciate all that they do for us.*

MUSIC: Think of a world without any flowers   JP254
Stand up, clap hands, shout thank you, Lord   JP225
He gave me eyes so I could see   JP74
(see also Mother's Day (1), and Father's Day (1) and (2))

THEME: *Nature*

AIM: For the children to appreciate that God, as Creator of Nature, wants us to love, appreciate and take care of, all that he has created.

AIDS: *A stone; an insect in a jar; a flower; a hamster, mouse or guinea pig in a cage. "Person" shaped cards or sheets of paper.*

BIBLE TEXT: *God said, "Let the land produce vegetation." And so it was . . . And God said, "Let the water teem with living creatures, and let birds fly above the earth." And God saw that it was good.* Genesis 1:11 & 20

LEADER: What is the difference between this stone and this flower? (*Question and discussion to draw out the fact that the stone does not grow and is lifeless.*)

What is the difference between this flower and this insect? (*Again draw out the fact that the insect can move around but the flower is static.*)

What is the difference between this insect and the hamster (mouse, or guinea pig)? (*Draw out the fact that the hamster is a "higher" life form.*)

We believe that God made all these things and men and women (*show the person-shaped cards.*)

Stone – flower – insect – animal – mankind; God has made a wonderful order in his creation. Mankind has been placed at the top, so that we can take care of all the other things. "God saw that it was good" . . . and so must we.

Now on the person-shaped cards that you have write these words: "Lord, help us to love and take care of your creation."

PRAYER FOCUS: *Thanksgiving for stones, flowers, insects, animals and ourselves) may we take care of God's creation.*

MUSIC: For the beauty of the earth   JP48/MP152
All things bright and beautiful   JP6/MP23
O Lord my God! when I in awe-some wonder
   JP179/MP506
(*see also Taking Care of our World, and Creation*)

Obedience

AIM: To show how it has always been difficult to obey, but God expects us to try.

AID: *An apple.*

LEADER: You see this apple, it was believed for hundreds of years it was an apple which Eve took from the tree in the Garden of Eden and gave to Adam. Actually if you read the story carefully it says, "fruit"; so it could have been a date tree, or a fig tree or some similar tree.

Have you ever played the game, as you walk along the pavement or path, of not walking on the cracks? (*Adapt the following as necessary.*) My little son said to me the other day, "You're not allowed to walk on the cracks (lines)." So I had to walk with care. In other games you can hear children say, "You're not allowed." That's because there are rules to be kept.

Or you might call on your friend and he or she says, "Sorry, I'm not allowed out." If your friend then slips out the back door, he or she is being disobedient. If your friend gets caught doing what is not allowed, he or she will be in trouble; which causes unhappiness.

God wants us to be happy and if we keep the rules he has made – they are called the Ten

BIBLE TEXT: *You must not eat from the tree of the knowledge of good and evil.*   Genesis 2:17

Commandments – we will find it makes for a happier life than doing what we are not allowed.

PRAYER   *Adam and Eve's sin of doing what was not allowed*
FOCUS: *brought much unhappiness; may we try to obey God and*
              bring happiness into the lives of our family and friends.

MUSIC: Brothers and sisters   JP21
              I want to live for Jesus ev'ry day   JP122
              In our work and in our play   JP108
              (*see also The Commandments*)

Our Friend Jesus

AIM: To help the children view Jesus as a personal friend not as a distant, unapproachable being.

AIDS: *A picture or poster of Jesus.*

LEADER: Here is a picture, by an artist, of Jesus.

Is this a photograph? No. It is the artist's idea of how she or he thought Jesus looked.

Do we really know what Jesus looked like? No, actually we have no idea. No one, at the time of Jesus, took the trouble of describing him to us.

Do you think he looked like this picture?

Let's hear your ideas. Do you think he would be tall or short?

Would you think he had dark hair or blond hair?

What about his face? Was it a thin face or a round kind of face? Do you think Jesus was serious all the time or laughed a lot?

It's up to you and me to form in our own imagination a picture of Jesus.

One thing we do know for certain – he wants you and me to be his friend. How do we become his friend? He tells us in John's gospel, chapter 15. (Read from verse 9 to 17.)

BIBLE TEXT: *I have called you friends, for everything that I learned from my Father I have made known to you.* John 15:15

PRAYER
FOCUS: *Thankfulness for the privilege of being called "friend" by Jesus; may all our friends do what Jesus asks and become his friends too.*

MUSIC: What a friend we have in Jesus   JP273/MP746
Lord Jesus Christ   JP156/MP435
With Jesus in the boat   JP291
Jesus is a friend of mine   JP136
(*see also Jesus, and Christ – Human Like Us*)

Patience

AIM: To help the children appreciate the meaning and value of patience.

AIDS: *None.*

LEADER: Do your parents often say to you, "Be patient. Wait and take your time," or something like that?

A little Scottish girl was once asked, "What is patience?" In her Scottish accent she replied, "Wait a wee while, and dinna weary." That is a super way to explain patience. "Do not grow weary" she said, and that is the important part; wait but do not grow weary. Here is a story about patience.

Sir Isaac Newton was a famous scientist and he owned a dog called Diamond. Newton had taken eight whole years to write an important book. At last he finished his book and left it on his desk and went to bed. He was wakened by Diamond barking, and by smoke coming from his study. He rushed to put out the fire which had destroyed most of his desk . . . and the book. Isaac Newton had gone to bed, very tired, and left a candle burning on the desk. Diamond, his dog, had knocked the candle over and set fire to the book. "Diamond," said Newton, "you have no idea what trouble you have caused me." But there and then Newton sat down and started the book again.

BIBLE TEXT: *Do you want us to go and weed it out? But he said, "No, because when you weed out the darnel, you might pull up the wheat with it. Let them both grow till the harvest."*

Matthew 13:28

PRAYER
FOCUS:
Thankfulness for God's patience with us; help to be patient with other people.

MUSIC:
Father, I place into your hands   JP42/MP133
Be bold, Be strong, for the Lord your God is with
   you   JP14/MP49
I'll be still and know that you are God   JP93
(*see also Perseverance*)

Peace

AIM: To encourage the children to think about the meaning of peace in relationship with Christ, the Prince of Peace.

AIDS: *Prepare the children to go into the church, or wherever the service is to take place, and make a noisy disturbance, over who is going to sit in which seat. Perhaps arrange a pretend fight between two of the boys. (But only just before the leader is about to enter.)*

LEADER: What is all this noise about? (*Separate the two who are pretending to fight.*) Let's have some peace and quiet.

Now sit down quietly and listen to a story. There is a very big continent called South America and down at the narrow end of this continent there are two countries who are separated by a range of mountains called the Andes.

Standing on top of these mountains, between the two countries, is a huge statue of Christ. This is how the statue came to be put between the two countries.

Chile and Argentina were quarrelling over some land which both countries said was theirs. (Remember our disturbance at the beginning over the same type of thing.) They got ready for war; made lots of guns and trained soldiers for the coming war. BUT the Christian church leaders in both countries got together and began to plead for

Peace I leave with you; my peace I give you.

                        John 14:27

peace in the name of Christ. They went round and preached peace everywhere, and to all the important people. Peace won.

Instead of firing their guns both countries melted down the guns and used the metal to make a huge statue of Christ. They said that would remind them never to think of fighting one another again.

At the foot of the statue are these words:
"These mountains shall fall and crumble to dust before the people of Chile and Argentina shall forget their solemn, covenant sworn at the feet of Christ."

When there is a disturbance inside ourselves or between us let us always turn to Christ, our friend, and pray for peace.

PRAYER
FOCUS: *Gratitude for the peace that we enjoy in our country; prayer for refugees and the victims of disturbances around the world.*

MUSIC: I've got peace like a river   JP120/MP353
              Peace, I give to you   JP196/MP553
              Make me a channel of your peace   JP161/MP456

Pentecost (1)

AIM: To help the children have some appreciation of the meaning of this Christian festival.

AIDS: *An assortment of candles, as varied as possible: one tall and thin, one squat, one red, etc. To be arranged in full view.*

LEADER: Here, as you can see, I have a selection of candles. Some are small and some are tall, some are fat and some are thin. There are coloured ones and white ones, etc.

I am going to strike a match and light them all (*match action to words*).

Now let us think about what we can see. All the different candles burn with the same flame – you saw me light them all from the same match(es). All have the same size flame burning and if it were dark you would not see whether the candle was red or white; thin or fat and so on.

On the first Pentecost Day the Holy Spirit came. It did not matter whether the friend of Jesus, in that upper room, was tall and thin or short and fat; it did not matter whether the friend was a man or a woman. The same Spirit filled each equally.

There are different people in front of me now – some tall and some short; some one colour and some another. It does not matter to the Holy Spirit, who fills each regardless.

BIBLE TEXT: *They saw what seemed to be tongues of fire that separated and came to rest on each of them.* Acts 2:3

That is the point of Pentecost; the Holy Spirit gives value and worth to everyone. We are all equally possessed of the flame of life and we can all grow in faith and love.

PRAYER
FOCUS: *Thanksgiving for the gift of the Holy Spirit who gives us faith; help to grow in the gifts of the Holy Spirit.*

MUSIC: All over the world the Spirit is moving   JP5/MP18
Spirit of the living God fall afresh on me   JP222/MP613
Praise God from whom all blessings flow   JP199/MP557
(*see also Holy Spirit, and Pentecost (2)*)

THEME: *Pentecost (2)*

AIM: To help the children understand the signs of the Holy Spirit at work.

AIDS: *Enough balloons (they need to be tested with a pump before giving them out) to give one to each child. One large candle standing in a prominent position.*

LEADER: Today we think about a birthday. The birthday of the Christian Church.

Let's now blow up our balloons.

That was quite an effort. Your balloon now holds the air which has come from inside you. Now look carefully at your balloon, to make sure you will recognize it again. Let's all let our balloons go. Now go and find it. That was fun; but look at your balloon . . . it is sad and lifeless, quite wrinkled up. You see the air gave it a kind of life, a shape and a purpose.

That is exactly what happened on Pentecost Day: the Holy Spirit filled people who were lifeless; the Spirit gave shape to the community and gave them drive and purpose.

Now I am going to light this large candle that you can all see. The match flares and I light the candle (*match words to actions*).

You see that flame burning. If this room (church, etc.) were dark that candle would shine out and light up the room. That is another idea for us to

BIBLE TEXT: *They heard what sounded like a powerful wind from heaven . . . something appeared to them that seemed like tongues of fire.* Acts 2:2–3

think about today. The Holy Spirit lit up the darkness for the friends of Jesus; suddenly they understood and believed . . . and they had the courage to go out and tell others. When they did the Church began. Today the Church came alive.

PRAYER
FOCUS:
Thanks to God the Father for the gift of the Spirit, giving life and energy to the Church; may we too be filled with the same life and energy.

MUSIC:
God whose Son was once a man on earth   JP62/MP195
This is the day   JP255/MP691
Love, joy, peace and patience, kindness   JP158
(*see also Holy Spirit, and Pentecost (1)*)

THEME: *Perseverance*

AIM: To open the children's understanding to an appreciation of how some Christians have persevered in their faith.

AIDS: *A good reader.*

LEADER: Many, many Christians have had to endure great suffering for their Christian beliefs. Since the time of Jesus himself his followers have been persecuted. First there were sufferings caused by the Jewish leaders, then for a long period by the Roman emperors. It has gone on and on throughout history.

In the last hundred years or so the same thing has happened in China. Here is a poem from a Chinese Christian who suffered for his Christian beliefs about one hundred years ago.

READER: I am poor because I believe in the Lord,
My heart seems restless;
Yet once I think of the Lord, even though I tramp the roads,
My heart is happy.

I meet oppression because I study the true way,
My heart seems restless;
Yet once I think of the Lord, even though I am bound in chains,
My heart is happy.

We rejoice in our sufferings, because we know that suffering produces perseverance; perseverance, character; and character, hope.   Romans 5:3

I experience trials for the sake of the Gospel,
My heart seems restless;
Yet once I think of the Lord, even though I am beaten with whips,
My heart is happy
I am tortured for the sake of the Church,
My heart seems restless;
Yet once I think of the Lord, even though I am crucified,
My heart is so happy.
Lord give me peace, Lord give me peace.
The peace granted by the Lord is not that of worldly riches.
People cannot steal it from you, peace is in heaven.

LEADER: That moving poem was by Hsi Sin-Mor a Christian minister who persevered, that is kept going when everything seemed against him. If we too "keep going" in our Christian faith, no matter what the difficulties are, we too will find that our hearts are so happy.

PRAYER FOCUS: *Gratitude for the example of the heroic Christians of the past; help for Christians who are persecuted today and help for ourselves that we too may persevere.*

MUSIC: We shall overcome   JP270
Your hand, O God has guided   JP298
One more step along the world I go   JP188
(*see also Patience*)

Pets

AIM: To show the children that God is interested in their pets and all their interests.

AIDS: *Make and give out "animal shapes" of cats, dogs, fish, birds, etc. (Some research beforehand into the children's pets might be useful.) Pencils or crayons to write with. A reader.*

LEADER: You know the story of how God made the first man, Adam. According to the second and oldest story, found in the first book of the Bible, Genesis, God made the man all alone. Adam felt lonely so God looked for a friend for him. That is how God came to make the animals; as possible friends for Man.

READER: So God moulded all the wild animals and the wild birds – again, out of the ground itself. He led Man to them to see what names he would give them – these would be the names they would always be called by. Man gave names to all the domestic animals, the wild birds and the wild animals. (*A. Dale's Winding Quest*)

LEADER: Isn't that a lovely story? The man, Adam, did just the same as you do when you get a new pet; you give it a name, which shows that you have a special care for that animal.

God wants you to care for your pet and treat it kindly. Take these shapes – choose one that

---

BIBLE TEXT: *God brought the animals to the man to see what he would name them. So the man gave names to all the livestock, the birds of the air and all the beasts of the field.*

Genesis 2:19

reminds you of your pet (if you have more than one pet, just choose one shape).

On the back of the shape, write your pet's name (if you have more than one, write all their names). Now write the words "Thank you for my cat or dog or goldfish" on the back.

PRAYER
FOCUS: *Thanksgiving for our pets; help to look after them properly. Prayer for those who do not care for and respect animals.*

MUSIC: All things bright and beautiful   JP6/MP23
Have you seen the pussy cat, sitting on the wall?   JP72
Who put the colours in the rainbow?   JP288

Praise

AIM: To help the children appreciate the meaning of "praise" and how we need to praise God for his goodness.

AIDS: *The objects and "works of art" that the children have brought in, as requested the previous week. Also a large poster with the words, "Lord we admire and praise you for this world that you have made."*

LEADER: Last week I asked you to bring this week something that you had made; it could be a picture you have painted or a model you have made or anything like that.

Let's see what we have (*admire and show what has been brought in*).

What a nice feeling it is when people admire what we have made. These things you have made have taken time and skill.

Let us stop and think about God for a moment. What is it that we believe he has made? Yes, this beautiful world in which we live. He likes to be admired and praised for what he has made. Let us now say together:

"Lord we admire and praise you for this world that you have made" (*poster is held to view*).

BIBLE TEXT: *Praise the Lord, O my soul*
all my inmost being, praise his holy name.
Psalm 103

PRAYER
FOCUS:
Thankfulness for this beautiful world; praise to God who made it. That we may constantly admire and praise God for his goodness.

MUSIC:
Clap your hands all you people   JP26
From the rising of the sun   JP49/MP163
Praise him, praise him   JP202
Praise him on the trumpet   JP200/MP558

THEME: *Prayer*

AIM: To help the children think more deeply about prayer and appreciate the need for it.

AIDS: *A simple object, hidden for the children to find. Two posters: the first with the word ASK at the top of the sheet, then on the lower half the words AND YOU WILL RECEIVE. Fold the poster so that only the word ASK can be seen. Do the same with the words, SEEK, AND YOU WILL FIND.*

LEADER: If you would like your friend to come round to your house to play, what do you do?

Yes, you ask. You ask your parents and your friend also asks. (*Show the ASK poster and reveal the bottom half.*)

Now I have hidden a (thimble, marble, ball, etc.) over in this part of the church; get up and see who can find it. (*Hold up the SEEK poster and reveal the bottom part when the object is found.*)

Jesus tell us never to hesitate – if we need help we should ask our loving Father for it; and keep asking. Jesus says prayer is like seeking for something, you have to get up and make an effort but God, our loving Father, will reward our effort.

190

BIBLE TEXT: *Ask and you shall receive; seek and you will find; knock and the door will be opened to you.*   Luke 11:9

PRAYER
FOCUS:
Thank God for his fatherly love and interest in us; and his desire to help us. Help to always turn to God when we need him.

MUSIC:
Ask! Ask! Ask! and it shall be given you   JP11
It's me, it's me, it's me, O Lord   JP119
Kum ba yah, my Lord, Kum ba yah   JP149
(*see also Teach us to Pray, and The Lord's Prayer*)

THEME: *Prejudice*

AIM: To help the children to understand that "name-calling" and discriminatory actions are not the way for Christians to behave.

AIDS: *None.*

LEADER: Let me tell you a true story that appeared in a newspaper not long ago.

Robert was born in Aldershot; his mother was Japanese and his father was English, a soldier in the British Army. When Robert started school, because he had black hair and looked a little Japanese, he was tormented by the other children. One Christmas his parents gave him a watch. Robert was very proud of his present and wore it to school. His watch was taken from him by some older children and smashed against the school wall.

The school crossing warden asked Robert one day why he was walking to school, and crossing a busy road, when he could use the school bus. Robert told the warden that his parents wanted him to use the bus but he was frightened of the other children because they called him a "wog" and a "chink" and other very rude names. Robert walked to school for three weeks, until one day, when crossing the road, he was knocked down by a car and killed.

BIBLE TEXT: *I was a stranger and you invited me in.*
Matthew 25:35

Who killed Robert? Was it the car driver?

No, it was the other children; their name-calling forced Robert to walk to school and cross that busy road.

The name-calling killed Robert.

PRAYER
FOCUS: *That we may never forget the Lord's command that we love one another and remember that what we do to the least person we do to Christ himself.*

MUSIC: Make me a channel of your peace   JP161/MP456
Jesus died for all the children   JP132
There are hundreds of sparrows   JP246
(*see Dignity, and Special Person*)

Reading the Signs

AIM: To help the children appreciate that they have an opportunity to help their parents and friends at times of difficulty; in that way they are serving Christ.

AIDS: *Four young readers for the following:*

A. *Evening red and morning grey,*
   Send the traveller on his way;

   Evening grey and morning red
   Bring the rain upon his head.

B. *Mackerel sky,*
   Mackerel sky,
   Not long wet
   And not long dry.

C. *Rain, rain go to Spain,*
   Never show your face again.

D. *Red sky at night, shepherd's delight,*
   Red sky in morning, shepherd's warning.

LEADER: Each of the four short readings, rhymes about the weather that we have just had read to us, are traditional; that means that they have been around for a very long time and no one now knows who wrote them.

BIBLE TEXT: *Jesus replied, "When evening comes, you say, 'It will be fair weather, for the sky is red,' and in the morning, 'Today it will be stormy, for the sky is red and overcast.' You know how to interpret the appearance of the sky, but you cannot interpret the signs of the times."*

Matthew 16:1–3

Did you notice how they are almost exactly the same as the traditional rhyme that Jesus used?

At the time of Jesus they had no weather forecasts; they depended upon the signs that everyone could see. We ought to look out for signs; signs of what we could do to help. For example, sometime your mother or father, or whoever looks after you, are not feeling very well; or they are very tired. If you are alert you can recognize the signs – that is the sign that help is needed. We all know what it is to be ill or very tired and so you and I can easily offer to help at such a time. That is the love Jesus speaks about; in action, when it is most needed.

PRAYER   *That we may all look for the signs of where and when help*
FOCUS: *is needed and for the strength to offer to help.*

MUSIC: Rise, and shine, and give God his glory, glory   JP210
Jesus is knocking   JP135
I want to live for Jesus ev'ry day   JP122
(*see also Helpfulness and Helping*)

Risen Lord

AIM: To help the children appreciate the importance of believing and trusting the witnesses of the Resurrection.

AIDS: *A "feely bag" containing two or three objects, e.g. common objects from the kitchen: a whisk, a serving spoon, etc. A reader.*

LEADER: I would like you to pass this bag around (no one may look inside) and put your hand in and feel one of the objects. Then say, "I believe there's a . . . in this bag." I will go first. "I believe there is a tin box in this bag." Now we will pass it round and when you have finished we will see what is in the bag.

You have called out a number of different ideas; let us now see what is in the bag.

(*Identify the objects so that all may see.*) Now we know because we can see the objects.

When the tomb of Jesus on the first Easter morning was seen to be empty, his friends asked the question, "What has happened to the body of Jesus?" They did not believe until they had seen Jesus alive, there in front of them. But one would not believe, because he had not seen. Let's hear that story now.

READER: That Easter evening one of the friends of Jesus was absent – Thomas, "the twin".

"We've seen the Master," the others told him when he came back.

"I don't believe it," he said. "I must see the nailmarks in his hands and touch them first – and I must put my hand in his side."

The following Sunday, the friends of Jesus were again in the house with locked doors. This time Thomas was there too.

Then – Jesus was with them again.

"Peace be with you," he said.

He turned to Thomas.

"Where are your fingers?" he said. "Here are my hands. Touch my side with your hand. You must show that you trust, not that you don't."

"My Lord and my God," said Thomas.

"Do you trust me," asked Jesus, "just because you have seen me with your own eyes? They are happy people who trust me, without ever having seen me with their own eyes." (*A. Dale*)

LEADER: Jesus is talking about you and me at the end of that story. We have not seen the risen Jesus with our own eyes, but we trust what the friends saw and tell us they saw.

PRAYER
FOCUS:
Thankfulness for a Lord and Master who is always with us; intercession for those who do not believe in the raising of Jesus from the dead.

MUSIC: Alleluia, Alleluia, give thanks to the risen Lord   JP3/MP30
He is Lord   JP75/MP220
I serve a risen Saviour   JP113/MP295
(*See also Easter (1) and Easter (2)*)

Rules

AIM: To help the children understand that rules are necessary and God does expect us to obey, just as his son did.

AIDS: *A few road signs, reproduced on card or large sheets of paper, e.g. STOP sign and ONE WAY street sign, etc.*

LEADER: (*Hold up a road sign*) Does anyone know what this sign says? Yes, it means that the car must stop. (*Or whatever*.) Here are some more signs; what do they say? The signs tell drivers what they are allowed to do and what they are not allowed to do.

What would happen if there were no road signs? No rules for drivers? Yes, there would be chaos and lots of people would be hurt. So the rules are there to protect people.

Are there rules to be kept at home? There were rules in the family Jesus grew up in, because the Gospel tells that he went home and was obedient; that means he kept the rules that Mary and Joseph had in their home.

The rules in your home are there to protect you and help you to grow up to be the balanced, kind person God wants you to be.

BIBLE TEXT: *Jesus went down to Nazareth with Mary and Joseph and was obedient to them.* Luke 2:51

PRAYER FOCUS: *Thanksgiving for the road signs and rules that keep us safe; help to keep the other rules there are at home and at school.*

MUSIC: God is our guide, our light and our deliverer   JP56
Father, I place into your hands   JP42/MP133
Father, lead me day by day   JP43
(see also The Commandments, and Obedience)

THEME: *Saints*

AIM: To help children realize that all Christians are called to be saints of God; and we should support one another in that calling.

AIDS: *One A4 size imitation stained glass window, sold in English cathedral bookshops (if available and thought desirable).*

LEADER: Hands up those who have visited a cathedral; perhaps Salisbury, York, Canterbury or Durham.

What do you see in all cathedrals? Here is a clue (*show the imitation stained glass*).

Here is a story about a little girl who visited a big old cathedral for the first time.

The little girl was with her family in a party being shown round the cathedral. As the guide was explaining a historic tomb nearby, the girl was staring at a great stained glass window, through which the summer sun was streaming, bathing the cathedral floor in colour. As the group was about to move on she asked the guide in a shrill clear voice, "Who are those people in the pretty window?"

"Those are the saints," the man replied. That night as she was undressing for bed she told her mother, "I know who the saints are."

"Do you dear?" replied her mother, "who are they?"

BIBLE TEXT: *Be alert and always keep on praying for all the saints.*
                                                    Ephesians 6:18

'They're the people who let the light shine through."

We do not know what the mother said in reply but she could have reminded her little daughter that to let Christ's light shine through us is the calling we all have as Christians.

PRAYER   *Thanksgiving for the shining example of Christians of the*
FOCUS: *past; help to be the sort of Christians that Christ's light*
             shines through.

MUSIC: I sing a song of the saints of God   JP115
             O when the saints go marching in   JP195
             Your hand, O God has guided   JP298

THEME: *Salvation*

AIM: To make the word and concept of "salvation" understandable to children.

AIDS: *Cardboard "shackles" made to attach to each "slave", either round the legs or the neck. Alternatively, the slaves can come into view one behind the other in a line, heads bent and their left arms extended, hand on the shoulder of the "slave" in front.*

LEADER: Today I want to talk about slavery (*With these words the line of five or six "slaves" appears and shuffles towards the leader.*)

Slavery was abolished by our country in 1833 (*at these words the "slaves" drop their left arms to their sides and give a little cheer*). But today there are over 200 million slaves in the world. (*The slaves groan, "Oh No" and resume their "slavery" posture. They continue until they are close to the speaker and sit down on the floor.*)

Let me tell you the true story about one of today's slaves; her name is Binlah.

We should no longer be slaves to sin.
Romans 6:16

Binlah is now free and happy but when she was eleven-years-old she became a slave. Binlah lived with her family in a village called Korat in north-east Thailand. They were very poor, so when a smartly dressed business man from Bangkok arrived by car they were very interested to hear of the work he could get for Binlah in the big city. Assured that she would be cared for and have a good job in a restaurant, Binlah's father accepted £85 for her.

In Bangkok, three hundred miles from home, Binlah was re-sold by the agent at a profit to the owner of an ice cream factory. She was shown the machine that she had to work on and the dirty mattress alongside it, where she was to sleep. She had to start work at five in the morning and did not finish until midnight. She receives one meal a day and had to eat and sleep where she worked.

Later she told how the man would hit her to make her work faster; and how she cried herself to sleep each night. Fortunately for Binlah her mattress was beside the corrugated sheeting which formed the wall of the factory and her crying each night could be heard by a poor family close to the factory. They alerted a representative of the Save the Children Fund. The Fund arranged to buy back the brutally beaten and half-starved eleven-year-old.

Binlah was returned to her family. What an evil is

slavery. The Save the Children Fund saved the life of Binlah; if they had not bought her back she would have been dead within a year.

You have heard how we call Jesus our Saviour; he did for us what the Save the Children Fund did for Binlah; Jesus paid the price of his own blood to free us from the slavery that comes from doing wrong.

PRAYER
FOCUS:

Thank you to Jesus for the love he shows each of us by paying such a high price to make us free.

MUSIC: I have decided to follow Jesus   JP98/MP272
                    Oh! Oh! Oh! how good is the Lord   JP180/MP532
                    We have heard a joyful sound!   JP266/MP730

THEME: *School*

AIM: To help the children appreciate that school is not just imposed on them; Jesus went to school and "grew in wisdom", as must they.

AIDS: *None.*

LEADER: Who likes going to school? Yes, some children do and some children are not so keen.

Did you realise that Jesus went to school? Schools were very different then. First of all only the boys went to school; the girls still had to learn, but they learnt the household skills and how to prepare for and celebrate the great Jewish festivals in the home.

The boys went to a place called 'the house of the book". Can anyone guess what "book" they were talking about? Yes, the first five books of the Hebrew Bible.

Jesus would have gone to this place, which was usually part of the local synagogue, from the age of six. He would have sat with the other boys in a semi-circle on the floor at the feet of the teacher. Most of the teaching and learning was done by reciting together the lessons and learning them by heart.

They were taught how to read the Hebrew of the Bible and how to write. This was done in wax on a wood slate or perhaps, if the school was rather poor, in the dust of the floor. Jesus probably went to

BIBLE TEXT: *Jesus grew in wisdom and stature, and in favour with God and men.*   Luke: 1:52

school until he was 15 so he was quite well educated for that time. He probably knew more languages than you do. He would know his own local village version of Aramaic, he would have learnt Hebrew in the local school and he would know some common Greek from visiting the markets where the travelling traders would have spoken Greek.

So going to school is important and like Jesus we should do our best so that we too grow in wisdom.

PRAYER
FOCUS: *Gratitude for our schools and our teachers; help to work hard and grace to grow in wisdom as the years pass.*

MUSIC: Have you seen the pussy cat, sitting on the wall?   JP72
Father, lead me day by day   JP43
Children of Jerusalem   JP24/MP70

THEME: *Sharing*

AIM: To help children understand that growing up as a Christian involves learning to share.

AIDS: *None, unless in the appropriate setting the story can be mimed by older children.*

LEADER: Two-year-old Sharon and her friend Michael, who was nearly four, were playing happily in the garden.

Suddenly their mums, who were enjoying a quiet cup of coffee in the kitchen, were disturbed by a great commotion. Rushing to the window they saw both children trying to jam themselves, at the same time, on to the seat of the one and only small tricycle. After much shouting and screeching both managed to squeeze on, but neither could move. When their mums got to them Sharon was sobbing and Michael was stoutly and loudly proclaiming, "If one of us got off I could ride it properly."

It was resolved that they would take turns. Michael had the first short ride up the concrete garden path, pursued after less than thirty seconds by Sharon, calling, 'Me turn, me turn."

BIBLE TEXT: *If anyone has two tunics he must share with the man who*
               has none.   Luke 3:10

PRAYER   *Thanksgiving for the daily opportunity to share, at home,*
FOCUS: *at school and at play; help to be generous in sharing what*
               we have and what we do.

MUSIC: When I needed a neighbour were you there, were
                  you there?   JP275
               Make me a channel of your peace   JP161/MP456
               A boy gave to Jesus five loaves and two fish   JP1

Sight

AIM: For the children to appreciate their God-given sense of sight.

AIDS: *A pin and a sheet of paper for each child.*

LEADER: Do you ever play the game "I spy with my little eye." Let's play it for a minute or two.

I spy with my little eye something beginning with L.

Now look around and see if you can spy from my clue the object I noticed just now.

Yes, well done, L for lights. Now it is your turn.

Now I would like you to take a pin and a piece of paper and while I am telling you a story prick out with little pin holes a picture of a house, or a flower or a car or any picture you would like.

Here is the story: A small French boy named Louis, in the year 1809, had a terrible accident. His father was a harness-maker and they lived in a village near Paris. Louis's father put down a sharp tool on his work bench and left the workshop for a few moments. While he was away his young son thought that he would imitate his father; he picked up the tool, it slipped and went into his eye. It was very very painful. The infection from his blinded eye spread to the good eye and he became blind in both eyes.

BIBLE TEXT: *"Jesus put mud on my eyes," the man replied, "and I washed, and now I see."* John 9:15

Louis went to a special school and became very good with his hands. Later he invented an alphabet made up of raised dots which can be "read" with the touch of the blind person's fingers. It was named after him, Louis Braille.

Now if everyone has finished their pictures, close your eyes and pass the paper along to someone else. When you have received a sheet of paper, without looking, turn the sheet over and feel the pattern or picture. Can you find out what the picture is just by touch?

You can now look to see if you were correct. Braille is rather like that; it is made up of raised dots which can be felt and "read" with the fingers.

Let us always thank God for the gift he gives us of sight.

PRAYER FOCUS: *Thankfulness for the God-given gift of sight; help for those who are born blind or who lose their sight in an accident or through disease.*

MUSIC: I have seen the golden sunshine   JP99
He gave me eyes so I could see   JP74
Two little eyes to look to God   JP262

211

THEME: *Special Person*

AIM: To give the children an insight of their specialness to God; their unique human dignity.

AIDS: *A model-making kit. This could be anything like a ship, a plane, etc.*

LEADER: I have here (open the kit box and hold up the plastic parts) all I need to make a model. It is a good hobby that entertains many people, young and old. This kit is one of thousands, exactly the same, made in a factory somewhere.

Now we come to the thumb test. Everyone hold your thumb for me to see, either hand. (*Look at own thumb*) now let's look at that thumb. Can you see all the little lines, your thumb print? That print is unique; that means your thumb is the only one in the world; there has never been a thumb like that before and there never will be; your thumb, the whole of you is specially made.

Let's read the passage from the Bible again.

I praise you because I am fearfully and
    wonderfully made;
your works are wonderful,
I know that full well.
My frame was not hidden from you
when I was made in the secret place.

BIBLE TEXT: *You created my inmost being;*
You knit me together in my mother's womb.

Psalm 139:13

Isn't that wonderful? God knew me, each of us, before we were even born, before we came out into the world. Each of us is a special and unique creation of God. We are not like this model here, run off by the thousands in a factory. God made me to be special.

PRAYER
FOCUS:
Thanksgiving for the wonder of my creation; a special unique person, made to know, love and serve God. Help for my parents who worked with God in my creation.

MUSIC:
If I were a butterfly   JP94
He gave me eyes so I could see   JP74
For the beauty of the earth   JP48/MP152
(*see also Dignity*)

THEME: *Sunday*

AIM: To encourage the children to think of Sunday as a
           special family day.

AIDS: *Two placards, one saying "Shopping" the other*
           "Working". A poster with the words "Keep holy the
           Sabbath day". Three placard/poster carriers.

LEADER: I am sure you have heard that some people want the
           shops to open on Sundays; they say people should
           be free to go shopping if they want to. (*Placard*
           carrying word "Shopping" brought out on view.) There
           we are, "shopping" is what some demand.

           What will that mean for a large number of
           people? Yes, it will mean that if you have a job in a
           shop you will have to work. So some want to be free
           to work on Sundays. (*Placard carrying "Working" is*
           brought out; they stand side by side. The poster carrier
           now comes out but does not yet show the wording of the
           poster.)

           The questions that we, as Christians, should ask
           is, what does God want? What does God want us to
           do? What does God say about this? (*Poster carrier*
           pushes between the placards and says, "God says, 'Keep
           holy the Sabbath Day'.")

           But, we do not keep holy the Sabbath day do we?
           Because the Sabbath is actually Saturday and that is
           the day that the Jewish religion keeps holy; we keep
           the next day holy – Sunday. Does anyone know

BIBLE TEXT: *Observe the Sabbath, because it is holy to you.*
Exodus 31:14

why we keep Sunday holy and not Saturday? Yes, because that was the day on which Jesus rose from the dead. God wants us to keep one day special as a day of rest, a day when we worship God and spend time with our families.

PRAYER
FOCUS:

Thankfulness for one special day a week for time set aside for God and for our family; help for those who campaign to keep Sunday special.

MUSIC:

Morning has broken JP166/MP467
This little light of mine JP258
New every morning is the love JP171/MP480

THEME: *Taking Care of Our World*

AIM: To help the children understand that God has entrusted the welfare of our planet to us, to keep it safe.

AIDS: *A reader.*

LEADER: First I have a little story for you from China.

READER: A very old Chinese gentleman was busy in his orchard when the ruler of that district happened to pass by. "You are very old, surely," said the ruler.

"I have lived one hundred years," replied the old man.

"Indeed?" the ruler was impressed. "But are you not planting fruit trees?"

"I am," said the old man.

"My friend," murmured the ruler, "surely you do not hope to live long enough to gather the fruit from these young trees? And if not, why bother to make your back ache?"

"It is as you say," the gardener replied. "But sire, when I came into this world I found many good things awaiting me. I would like to think that when I pass on there will be good things waiting for others."

LEADER: That is just the point; we must take care of our world, because if we do not there will be nothing left for the children who come along after you; and after those children.

BIBLE TEXT: *Rule over the fish of the sea and the birds of the air and over every living creature that move on the ground.*

Genesis 1:28

PRAYER
FOCUS:

Thanksgiving for God's beautiful world; help to do all we can to keep our world for the people who will come after us.

MUSIC:

O Lord my God! when I in awe-some wonder
    JP179/MP506
Yes, God is good – in earth and sky   JP293/MP786
Who put the colours in the rainbow?   JP288
(see also Creation, and Nature)

THEME: *Teach Us to Pray*

AIM: To encourage the children to pray daily.

AIDS: *A flower in bloom (if possible one for each of the children).*

LEADER: You can see this beautiful flower (or, look at the lovely flower in your hand). Would anyone like to share any thoughts that you have looking at the flower?

       Yes, our world is a lovely place. It is God's gift to us; let's say thank you to him. "Dear God, thank you for this beautiful flower and all the lovely things you have created." (*Get the children to repeat the words.*)

       There, you have prayed. You could say a prayer like that by yourself.

       Jesus taught his friends how to pray and if we are serious friends of Jesus we never stop learning more and more about prayer. Let us now say together the prayer that he taught his friends. "Our Father . . ."

BIBLE TEXT: *Jesus was praying in a certain place. When he finished one of his disciples said to him, "Lord, teach us to pray."*

Luke 11:1

PRAYER FOCUS: *Thankfulness for the beauties of God's world; help to say "thank you" and to pray every day.*

MUSIC: Ask! Ask! Ask! and it shall be given you   JP11
All things bright and beautiful   JP6/MP23
Our Father who is in heaven   JP192/MP552

Time

AIM: To stimulate the children to think about time, and God as Lord of all time. (Only suitable for older children.)

AIDS: *An alarm clock; preferably an old-style, wind-up one with the big bells on the top. Set the alarm to ring a few minutes after the presentation begins. A reader.*

LEADER: "Hurry up, you'll be late."

"Come on, you're wasting time."

Have you ever had anything like this said to you before? Grown-ups are always talking about time, aren't they! Their lives seem to be ruled by the clock.

But have you ever wondered, what exactly is time?

Do you see this alarm clock. I have set it to ring in a few minutes' time.

What do we call time which has not yet come? The FUTURE. So some "time" in the future the alarm clock will ring.

What do we call time which is now? Yes, that is the PRESENT. So when you hear the alarm clock ringing that moment will be the present.

BIBLE TEXT: *There is a time for everything,*
and a season for every activity under heaven.

Ecclesiastes 3:1

What do we call time which is gone by? The PAST.
So in a little while – in the future the alarm clock will
ring. When it is ringing – that is the present. Then
we will talk about it ringing – and that will be the
past. While we are waiting for the alarm to ring we
will hear a poem about time.

READER: When as a child I laughed and wept – time crept.
When as a youth I dreamed and talked – time
walked.
When I became a full-grown man – time ran.
And later as I older grew – time flew.
Soon I shall find while travelling on – time gone.
Will Christ have saved my soul by then? Amen.

LEADER: Older people, like me, can understand the truth of
that verse. Time is mysterious. One wonderful
thought for you: we humans have future – present –
past in our lives. God has no future or past in his
life. He is the Lord of time, everything is NOW for
him; he lives in an eternal present.

(*Alarm rings, put it off after five or six seconds.*) No one
could miss that, could they? For five seconds we
heard the ring of the alarm – that was the present.
But now it has gone and we can remember the
sound – that is now in the past. So time is made up
of three parts FUTURE – while we waited for the
bell to ring; PRESENT – while it was ringing; PAST –

221

is now while we talk about the time when the bell was ringing.

For God there is no future and no past, just the NOW of the present. Not easy for me to explain, or for you to understand. It is important though not to waste such a precious thing as time . . . once it has gone it can never be brought back.

PRAYER   *Thankfulness for our lives and for the time God has given*
FOCUS: *us; may we use time well and not waste it.*

MUSIC: He's got the whole wide world in his hands   JP78/MP225
            I do not know what lies ahead   JP92/MP269
            I want to live for Jesus ev'ry day   JP122

Trinity –
Community of Love

AIM: To introduce the children to the difficult concept of
the unity of the three persons of the Godhead;
Tri-unity.

AIDS: *A large shamrock made out of card and coloured green.*
Three children of the same height and size (boys or girls,
not a mix). The "shamrock" needs to be hidden close to the
leader.

LEADER: Would my three volunteers come out and stand in a
circle, holding hands.

What links or joins up the three people we can
see? Yes their hands. In God there are three
persons: the Father, the Son and the Holy Spirit,
and they are united by something. What do you
think that is? Yes, love.

Look at our group of three and think of another
group that is united by love. Yes, the family. Father,
mother and child. (*Group return to their places.*)

It is very hard for me to explain to you how there
can be only God, but three persons in God. A
famous Christian called Patrick, over 1,500 years
ago, tried to explain the community of love, we call
the Trinity, to a crowd. He desperately looked
round to find something to help him (*match action*
with words) and picked up a leaf, which grows in
Ireland (where he was) and showed it to the people.

He said to them, "Is this a leaf?" and they all said

As soon as Jesus was baptized, he went up out of the water . . . he saw the Spirit of God descending like a dove . . . and a voice from heaven said, "This is my Son, whom I love."

Matthew 3:16

"Yes". He covered two parts, showing one part, and asked, "Is this a leaf?" (*Match action with words.*) And they answered "Yes". (*Repeat process for each of the "parts".*)

"So it is," said Patrick, "that the Father is God and the Son is God and the Holy Spirit is God; but (*holding up the shamrock*) there is only one God."

Difficult to understand? Yes, it is for me and for every other grown-up Christian. Even the cleverest person can never understand it properly; we believe because the Bible tells us that it is so.

PRAYER
FOCUS:
Gratitude for the love of Father, Son and Holy Spirit; help to live the Christian life in faith and trust.

MUSIC:
Father, we adore you   JP44/MP139
Father we love you   JP45/MP142
We really want to thank you Lord   JP268/MP734

THEME: *Trust in God*

AIM: To encourage the children to trust that Christ is
           always with them; and not to fear in time of trouble.

AIDS: *A large four-legged table; assorted ropes; a sheet or thin
           blanket; a cushion or pillow. One boy to play Jesus and
           several to be the disciples. A reader.*

LEADER: Before we read the story of the storm on the lake
           and then act it out, let us put a boat together. The
           table must be upside down and we need to tie the
           sheet (our sail) to one of the "masts". The cushion is
           put in one of the corners for "Jesus" to go to sleep
           on. Now let's hear the story, then our actors will
           perform it for us.

READER: Matthew 8:23–27. (*Text read.*)

LEADER: Now let us see our play. (*If prepared well beforehand
           the storm may be signalled by "thunder", "rainclouds",
           etc.*)

LEADER: Why did Jesus tell them not to worry? Yes, because
           although he was asleep he was there with them;
           there was no need to fear.
               We too must remember that when "storms"
           come in our lives Jesus is close by; he is always
           there even if to us he seems to be asleep. We must
           always trust in his presence with us.

BIBLE TEXT: *Jesus replied, "You of little faith, why are you so afraid?"*
Then he got up and rebuked the winds and the waves, and
it was completely calm.   Matthew 8:26

PRAYER   *Thankfulness for Christ, our friend, always being with*
FOCUS: *us; help to always remember this and trust.*

MUSIC: Be still and know that I am God   JP22/MP48
             Father, I place into your hands   JP42/MP133
             I am trusting you, Lord Jesus   JP86/MP258
             Will your anchor hold in the storms of life   JP290/MP770

THEME: *Truthfulness*

AIM: To get the children to think about the importance of being truthful and thereby trusted.

AIDS: *Have the proverb above written large on a placard or sheet. Also the proverbs*
"Individuals may perish; but truth is eternal" (French proverb)
"Time discovers truth" (Latin proverb)

LEADER: Here is a true story from a senior school.

A teacher of Religious Studies wanted to study truth and deceit with her class. At the end of a lesson she said,

"To prepare for our next lesson on truth and deceit I want you all to read chapter 17 of Mark's gospel."

The day of the next lesson came and the teacher asked,

"Who has done the homework that I set?"

All the hands went up.

"You," said the teacher, "are just the people who need this lesson about telling the truth, because there is no chapter 17 in Mark's gospel!"

The trouble with not telling the truth is that usually you get found out. (*Hold up and read out the Latin proverb.*)

"Time discovers truth." Truth cannot be changed, if something is true now it will always be

BIBLE TEXT: *Truthful lips endure forever, but a lying tongue lasts only a moment.*   Proverbs 12:19

true. (*Hold up and read out the French proverb.*)

"Individuals will perish but truth is eternal": that means that people are born and die but truth never changes. There is something wonderful about truth and something nasty about lies. (*Show Bible text.*)

What do you think happens if someone is always telling lies? That's right, no one can trust them; and that is what is so terrible about not telling the truth, people do not trust you.

PRAYER   *Thanksgiving for trust between people which is built upon*
FOCUS: *everyone telling the truth; help to always tell the truth*
             even if it is very hard.

MUSIC: Father, lead me day by day   JP43
             Put your hand in the hand of the man   JP206
             One more step along the world I go   JP188
             (*see also Trust in God*)

THEME: *Wonder*

AIM: To link the children's natural wonder about the world with God, the Creator.

AIDS: *A container of bubble mixture with the ring on a handle, for blowing bubbles. (A strong mix of water and washing-up liquid will do.)*

LEADER: I expect you have all done this before (*blows a stream of bubbles . . . take care to practise before hand to make sure the mixture works*).

What a wonderful stream of bubbles. Each is unique; that means that every bubble is different from every other bubble. See, there are large ones and small ones. Can you see the lovely colours? And then they burst and are gone. So simple but so beautiful. Snow is very similar. Each snowflake is unique, not like any other one; they drift down and are soon gone.

Here is a traditional story from the Africa.

In Amarli Bakoff's village when the time came for the young men to prove that they had come of age, they were sent off by the head man to search for the most beautiful thing in the world. They then had to return and show what they had found to the village elders. Amarli Bakoff raced off to the distant hills which had always fascinated him. He climbed higher and higher, up through the forest, across the scrubland and scrambled up the rocks to the snowline. He had never before seen snow.

BIBLE TEXT: *Your works are wonderful, I know that full well.*

Psalm 139:14

"Surely," he thought as he touched the dazzling whiteness, "this must be the most beautiful thing in the whole world." He plunged his hand into the stinging coldness and clutched a handful of the wonderful, pure snow.

With his hand held tightly closed he raced back to his village, eager to be back by the time the other youths returned. The villagers were already assembled in the square inspecting the priceless treasures which the other youths had discovered: jewels, silks, marvels of native craftsmanship, and many other things. Suddenly Amarli ran into the square. "What have you brought us?" the elders asked. "See," he cried triumphantly – and he opened his hand. There was nothing there. They saw nothing. Only Amarli Bakoff knew the meaning of what had happened. "The most beautiful thing in the world," he said, "is what the eye cannot see and what the hand cannot hold".

PRAYER
FOCUS:

Gratitude for the wonders of God's beautiful world; may we all be filled with wonder at the beauty of God's creation, and respect and take care of our world.

MUSIC:

O Lord my God! when I in awe-some wonder
JP179/MP506
It's a happy day and I praise God for the weather   JP118
Who put the colours in the rainbow?   JP288
(*see also Creation*)

THEME: *Words*

AIM: To encourage young children to ask questions about their Christian faith, and so grow in it.

AIDS: *None.*

LEADER: A little while ago on a winter's day a young girl came into my home and said, "The puddles outside are all ice-o-lated." I laughed; and she was immediately upset. I quickly explained that I was not laughing at her, but she had misused a word. She had meant to say, "the puddles outside are frozen"; the word "isolated" means something different. It means, left on its own.

Every day we hear children, and sometimes adults, using words in the wrong way. Words carry meaning and the wrong word can carry the wrong meaning.

Here, at this moment, I have ideas in my head. I want you to have the same ideas in your head, so I make sounds – which are words – which you hear and, I hope, understand. If I use the wrong word, then you do not get my meaning; if I use a word you do not understand, again you do not get my meaning.

In church we very often use special words that you will not hear when playing with your friends. For example, "salvation" "redemption" "grace" and so on.

BIBLE TEXT: *Do not merely listen to the word, and so deceive yourselves. Do what it says.*   James 1:22

God wants everything to be clear and plain to everyone; that is why his Son is called "the Word of God". Because we use very adult and churchy words, very often, you must ask if you do not understand the meaning of a word or words being used.

PRAYER
FOCUS: *Thanksgiving for the gift of speech and hearing; courage to ask when we do not understand.*

MUSIC: Your ways are higher than mine   JP295
                Ask! Ask! Ask! and it shall be given you   JP11
                He gave me eyes so I could see   JP74

Worrying

AIM: To reassure the children that we have no need to worry because we are in God's hands.

AIDS: *None.*

LEADER: Today we have story about a man who went on holiday in Cornwall. In that part of England there use to be a large number of mines, now disused. Some of the mineshafts are not filled in and have no rails around them.

The man in our story went out for a long walk one day and got lost; it became dark and he stumbled on. In spite of his care he slipped and started sliding down a mineshaft. He managed to cling on to a rock as he was sliding down and hung on. He was terrified and prayed aloud, "Lord help me!" Time passed and his arms ached so much that he felt he would not last much longer, when he heard a shout in the distance and the beam of a flashlight cut through the dark. He started shouting as loud as he could. When the rescuers arrived and shone their torches down on him, the first thing they saw was that the trapped man was dangling only a few inches from solid ground. The mineshaft had been filled in and he had suffered an agony of worry unnecessarily.

The man worried and there had been no need to

BIBLE TEXT: *I tell you, do not worry about your life.*
                                        Matthew 6:25

worry. We often worry about things and they are never as bad as we think. We must always pray and really trust God.

PRAYER   *Thankfulness that God is always close at hand; that we*
FOCUS: *may believe so deeply in God's love for us that we will*
              place ourselves into his hands and learn not to worry.

MUSIC: Will your anchor hold in the storms of life   JP290/MP770
              Make me a channel of your peace   JP161/MP456
              How great is our God! How great is his name
                  JP82/MP245
              (*see also Anxiety and Trust in God*)

SCRIPTURE INDEX

THE OLD TESTAMENT

THE NEW TESTAMENT